A first course in computer programming using C

A first course in computer programming using C

Melvyn King
John Pardoe
Paul Vickers

The McGraw-Hill Companies

London • New York • St Louis • San Francisco • Auckland • Bogotá
Caracas • Lisbon • Madrid • Mexico • Milan • Montreal
New Delhi • Panama • Paris • San Juan • São Paulo • Singapore
Sydney • Tokyo • Toronto

Published by
McGraw-Hill Publishing Company
Shoppenhangers Road, Maidenhead, Berkshire SL6 2QL, England
Telephone 01628 23432
Fax 01628 770224

British Library Cataloguing in Publication Data
King, Melvyn
  First course in Programming Using C.
  I. Title
  005.133

D.C. 3·10·97
ISBN 0-07-707913-2

Library of Congress Cataloging-in-Publication Data

King, Melvyn (Melvyn Joseph),
  A first course in computer programming using C / Melvyn King, John Pardoe, Paul Vickers.
    p. cm.
  Includes bibliographical references and index.
  ISBN 0-07-707913-2
  1. C (Computer program language) 2. Electronic digital computers – Programming. I. Pardoe,
    John (John Phillip),
  II. Vickers, Paul. III. Title.
QA76.73.C15K5   1994
005.13'3 – dc 20   94-21220 CIP

McGraw-Hill

*A Division of The **McGraw·Hill** Companies*

45 BL 976

Typeset by Focal Image Ltd, London
Printed and bound in Great Britain by
Biddles Limited, Guildford and King's Lynn

Printed on permanent paper in compliance with ISO Standard 9706

Contents

Preface   ix

1.   **Introduction to programming concepts**   **1**
     1.1   What is a computer program?   1
     1.2   Programming languages   1
     1.3   Using data in a computer program   2
     1.4   Repeating things and making decisions   3

2.   **Getting started**   **4**
     2.1   Running a program   4
     2.2   Operating systems, compilers and editors   5
     2.3   How to use the course material   6
     2.4   A first program   7
     Exercises   10

3.   **Declarations and assignments for integer numbers**   **12**
     3.1   The concept of data types   12
     3.2   Constant declarations   12
     3.3   Variable declarations   13
     3.4   Assignment statements   13
     3.5   The data type integer   17
     3.6   Integer output   19
     Exercises   21

4.   **Real numbers**   **24**
     4.1   The data type `float`   24
     4.2   Real expressions   25
     4.3   Output of real values   26
     Exercises   29

5.   Input and output   **31**
    5.1   Introduction   31
    5.2   Writing to the monitor screen   32
    5.3   Reading from the keyboard   34
    5.4   Interactive input and output   34
    5.5   Using data files   35
    Exercises   37

6.   Selection   **41**
    6.1   The `if` and `if-else` statements   41
    6.2   Relational operators   42
    6.3   Compound expressions   43
    6.4   Nested selections   48
    6.5   Compound statements   49
    Exercises   51

7.   Repetition   **55**
    7.1   The `while` statement   55
    7.2   Nested control structures   59
    Exercises   61

8.   Characters and strings   **66**
    8.1   The data type `char`   66
    8.2   Strings   70
    Exercises   76

9.   More control statements   **80**
    9.1   The `for` statement   80
    9.2   The `do-while` statement   83
    9.3   The `switch` statement   84
    Exercises   87

10.   Functions   **93**
    10.1 The function call   93
    10.2 The function definition   95
    10.3 Function parameters and arguments   98
    10.4 Scope   105
    10.5 Program development using functions   107
    Exercises   108

11.   Testing and debugging   **114**
    11.1 What is testing?   114
    11.2 Checking for syntax errors   114
    11.3 Manual testing for logical errors   115

11.4 Computer testing   115
11.5 Creating test data cases   115
11.6 Correcting errors (debugging)   116
11.7 Using a debugging tool   117
Exercises   117

12. An introduction to program design   122
12.1 High-quality software   122
12.2 Design objectives   123
12.3 Design constructs   124
12.4 A straightforward problem   125
12.5 A data processing problem   127
12.6 A more complex problem   129
Exercises   134

13. Introduction to arrays   137
13.1 The need for arrays   137
13.2 Arrays in C   138
13.3 Table look-up   141
13.4 Strings as arrays   142
Exercises   143

14. Multi-dimensional arrays   145
14.1 Examples of multi-dimensional arrays   145
14.2 Step-by-step guide to using arrays   149
Exercises   153

15. Type definitions   157
15.1 Fundamental data types   157
15.2 The use of `typedef`   158
15.3 Enumerated types   159
Exercises   161

16. Structures and unions   164
16.1 Structures   164
16.2 Unions   171
Exercises   172

17. Files   175
17.1 Streams   175
17.2 Input and output functions   175
17.3 End of file   179
Exercises   181

18.   Software units   **183**
         18.1 The preprocessor   183
         18.2 Macros   185
         18.3 Writing large programs   185
         Exercises   190

19.   Dynamic data structures   **191**
         19.1 Pointers   191
         19.2 Stacks   192
         19.3 Queues   200
         19.4 Ordered linked lists   205
         Exercises   211

Appendices

1.   Solutions to exercises   **215**
2.   An exercise using an editor program   **233**

Index   **239**

Preface

The aim of the course

The aim of this book is to provide a first course in the use of a methodical and effective approach to the development of computer programs using the programming language C.

It provides a foundation for those who wish to write high-quality computer programs based on sound design principles. The emphasis throughout is on good design practice and coding style. As it is a first course, no previous experience of computer programming is assumed.

Because this book is intended to be a primer, it deals with sufficient of the C language to allow the beginner to become comfortable with basic programming tasks. Of course, C is a versatile language and includes many features that are not directly addressed in this course, features which, in the authors' opinion, are out of reach of the novice. Thus the emphasis is always on helping the reader to understand sound principles of programming practice. On completing this course, the reader will be well equipped to proceed to texts dedicated to covering the entire C language.

Therefore, the text is suitable for first courses in programming at many levels such as GNVQ and A level, BTEC national and higher national courses, and degree. It is also suitable for the independent learner who is not enrolled on a formal programme of study.

C is gaining wider popularity in both industry and education, hence the need for an introductory text such as this. There are now several variations of the language on the market. ANSI C is used in this course because it is a standard language that all C compiler systems can recognize.

Content and structure

The course is a self-contained package. It starts with an introductory chapter on general programming concepts. Chapter 2 explains how to use the course material so that the reader can then run a simple program. Chapters 3 to 9 concentrate on the use of specific data types, namely integer and real numbers, characters and strings, and the control constructs that C provides for selection and repetition (iteration). The use of functions and aspects of testing and error removal (debugging) are then introduced in Chapters 10 and 11. Chapter 12 defines the characteristics of high-quality software and the objectives of a design method. An informal approach to producing pseudocode is also described. Chapters 13 to 17 examine the use of data structures, type definitions and files in C. Chapter 18 deals with some of the issues surrounding separately compiled sub-programs. Finally Chapter 19 looks at dynamic data structures and how they can be used.

Throughout the book, straightforward examples are used to introduce and illustrate each new concept.

The course material

The chapters in the book have been kept short deliberately to minimize the amount of reading. Exercises are included at the end of each chapter. The MS-DOS-compatible disk supplied with the text contains material that will help in developing solutions to the practical programming exercises.

There are two types of exercise. The first type is a self-assessment question requiring only the use of pencil and paper. It is designed to reinforce major points by referring the reader back to specific sections of the chapter in question.

The second type of exercise involves writing a computer program. For these exercises an outline design indicating how the problem is to be solved is provided in the text and on the accompanying disk. This demonstrates to the reader how a solution to the problem in hand can be expressed in a form of structured English (pseudocode) before it is coded in C. It also enables the reader to concentrate on the syntax and use of the language without spending too much time working out how to solve the problem.

Input-data files are also supplied on the disk for some of these exercises. When attempting these exercises, in addition to the outline design, help is available in the form of 'cheat' files on the disk. The cheat system gives the reader access to specific parts of the coded solution without seeing the complete program. Thus, a student experiencing difficulty with a particular aspect of the solution can obtain some help and continue without having to refer to the whole answer. If necessary, the complete solution can be obtained by assembling the code from the cheat files and the outline design.

Answer pointers to both types of exercise are given in Appendix 1.

1

Introduction to programming concepts

1.1 What is a computer program?

A computer is constructed so that a long sequence of instructions can be held in its internal storage areas, and these instructions can be executed at speed without human help. Such a sequence of instructions is called a *program* (note the spelling here).

Typically, a computer program may take some data such as numbers, perform some manipulation of that data (including calculations and comparisons), and then produce some results in a form that can be understood by a human. Usually, we refer to the data as the program's *input* and the results as the program's *output*.

1.2 Programming languages

To use computers we need to write programs. What sort of language can we use for writing the instructions for a computer? What language(s) does the computer understand?

The earliest computers were programmed in machine code, that is, by giving instructions in a numerical form. This was fine for the computer, but not very good for the computer programmer! Such programs were difficult to understand and modify, and did not possess the features that helped people to solve the problems in which they were interested.

At the other extreme, writing programs in English is not yet practical because it is too large, subtle and ambiguous a language. We need a language that is concise and precise.

So we compromise and use a language that combines the legibility and generality of English with the directness and precision of machine code. We call such languages *high-level* programming languages. Examples of these are C, Pascal, BASIC, COBOL and FORTRAN.

One of the aims of this book is to impress upon the reader that writing a good program involves far more than just learning a programming language. We shall address the importance of using the language in a methodical way, after we have carefully designed a solution to the problem in hand.

The problem we are trying to solve by computer must be carefully defined. This is often referred to as the program *specification*. Having understood the specification, we can then design a solution to the problem. This outline design is included in our programs as the 'description' (see Fig. 2.1). We can then elaborate the design by producing high-level programming language components from it. This is known as the *coding* process and the resulting components, also called *statements*, are known as the program *code*. We now have a *source program* in the C language which, as will be explained in Chapter 2, needs to be translated into a form that the computer can understand.

1.3   Using data in a computer program

Every computer program manipulates data in some way to produce results. We need to be able to refer to items of data in a convenient way, so most programming languages allow the programmer to choose names for each item of data in a program.

Items of data can be said to be constant or variable. This means that either the data item stays the same (has the same value) for the duration of the program execution or it is likely to take on a range of different values. Either way it is convenient to be able to identify the items of data. Therefore we use the terminology *identifiers*, *constants* and *variables*, where an identifier is the name of an item of data that may be constant or variable.

For example, in a program we may calculate the area of a circle of any given radius. We need a variable to hold the value of a radius, we need a variable to hold the result (which will be different for every different radius), and we need a constant for the value of π to an agreed level of accuracy (because this never changes).

Sometimes we need to group items of data together. In such cases we might give a name to the group as well as the individual items. For example, if we collected information about every student in the class, then for each student we would have a group of data items, known as a *record*, that we could identify as student_record. As part of the group we might have fields or items identified as name, age, address and so on.

The names given to identifiers should not be confused with the values of the data that the identifiers contain. We could identify a constant by giving it a name of say, twenty, but its permanent value might be 320! This is not a good idea. We could identify a variable by the name page_number with a value of zero to start with. Then as the program produces new pages of output, we can increase it to one, then two, then three and so forth.

Variable and constant data can be of different types. For instance, if we wanted to give values that are whole (integer) numbers, we would give a name to a variable and declare that its type is integer. If we wanted to give values that are several alphabetic characters such as for a person's name, we would need to declare a variable of the appropriate type.

1.4   Repeating things and making decisions

Most often in computer programs we will require the same set of instructions to be executed for many items of data. For instance, if we were processing the payroll for a company with twenty thousand employees, we might have a set of instructions to calculate tax that would be used repeatedly for all those employees who were subject to tax.

Programming languages allow us to write sections or blocks of code such that they may be repeated several times. This repetition may be for a fixed number of times, if we know how many. Or we may not know how many times we need to repeat the block; we only know we wish to execute it while a particular condition holds true or until another condition has been met. In computer terms we have just described *looping*, a process of repeating blocks of instructions.

Sometimes, we need to be selective about which blocks of instructions are executed (not all employees pay tax). So, we also have the facility to construct *conditions* that test the values of certain items of data. Depending on the outcome of the test we can either execute or skip over a certain block of instructions. Alternatively, it may be that there are several different blocks of instructions, each of which is for a particular purpose depending on certain data values. For example, if each employee had the choice of which trade union to join it might be that there would be different calculations of dues, each requiring a different block of instructions.

The programming language C has specific facilities that enable us to implement the general concepts outlined above. Many of these, with associated programming techniques, will be gradually introduced throughout this book.

2

Getting started

2.1 Running a program

As mentioned in Chapter 1, a source program cannot be understood directly by the computer; it must first be translated into an equivalent program in the machine language (code) of the computer. The machine code program is known as the *object program*.

This process of translation, known as *compilation*, is performed by a program stored within the computer called a *compiler*. So the compiler produces an object program that is then stored in computer memory, but it will only do this if there are no mistakes in the way you have used the language. If there are *syntax errors*, that is, mistakes in the C grammar, then the compiler will produce error messages.

Once we have produced a program without syntax errors and therefore have an object program in computer storage, the next stage, execution, may start. The computer executes the machine code instructions and may produce the results you require. However, at this stage further errors can occur. *Run-time* (or *execution*) errors occur when the programmer has made a mistake that was not a syntax error, but still contravenes the computer's rules (for example, trying to divide a number by zero). In such cases an appropriate run-time error message is produced.

Logical errors occur even when there are no syntax or run-time errors. The symptoms for these errors are results that are not as expected. The outline design may be wrong, or they may arise because the programming language statements are misused or are in the wrong order.

The error messages will help us to find the syntax and run-time errors. Detecting logical errors can obviously be more difficult. It is vitally important that we *test* our program, possibly with a range of data values, known as *test data*, to ensure that it works according to its specification. The task of finding out why a program is not working to specification is called *debugging*. This is because logical errors in programs are called *bugs*.

If we discover that the program is not correct for any reason, then we can change the contents of the source program using a special-purpose program known as an *editor*.

2.2 Operating systems, compilers and editors

An operating system is the program that is always resident in a computer and is used for controlling all of the actions of the computer, including those necessary for taking care of computer files and compiling and running programs. Most users of C will use the operating system called Unix or the PC operating system MS-DOS. The details of the ways that the user may invoke the facilities of the operating system are outside the scope of this book. However, the reader will need to be familiar with:

- The basic use of directories and files
- Copying and deleting files
- Displaying and printing file contents

The various C compilers also differ in the way in which they are used. Some are used as stand-alone programs, while others are fully integrated within a program development environment that includes an editor, file management facilities and many other options. Do not be overawed by a large number of options; you can get started by understanding a small number of these, for example:

- How to run the compiler and compile your programs
- How to run your programs once they have been successfully compiled

Most editor programs have many similar features, such as being able to insert new lines into a file, or delete characters from a file. The features that you are advised to become proficient with are:

- Moving the cursor
- Deleting text
- Inserting text

In addition it will be beneficial to become familiar with:

- Moving and copying text
- Replacing multiple occurrences of text
- Inserting the contents of other files into the file you are working with

To give you some idea of the way in which editors work, an exercise for you to practise on your editor is given in Appendix 2.

2.3   How to use the course material

The chapters have been kept quite small, so that there is a minimal amount of reading. Each chapter introduces a topic which is explained by examples. The examples should be studied carefully.

At the end of most chapters there are two types of exercise. The first type of exercise is a self-assessment one, which refers the reader back to the chapter to reinforce the major points. The only tools needed to do such exercises are pencil and paper. Answer pointers to the self-assessment exercises are given in Appendix 1.

The second type of exercise involves writing a computer program. Early on, you are provided with a lot of help for very simple problems; then, as you progress through the book, there may be less help and the exercises will get more difficult.

For the second type of exercise, the problem is specified in the text and, in most cases, an outline design is provided both in the text and in a file on the supplied disk in the EXERCISE directory. In tackling these exercises, the first thing you should do is read the problem carefully to understand what is required of the computer program. Next you should examine the outline design to determine how the problem is to be solved. Figure 2.1 shows the outline design for an exercise at the end of this chapter. Please ignore for the moment the first four lines and consider the next five. The first of these introduces the outline design with the word Description. Next we have three design statements. Normally one design statement will be used to produce one or more lines of program code. If you have understood the program requirements and the outline design you should be able to write down the C program code necessary.

At this stage, you should make a copy of the appropriate exercise file on another disk. Such files have names of the form EXccnn.C, where cc refers to the chapter number and nn refers to the exercise number within the chapter.

You should now use an editor program to change your own copy of the exercise file by inserting the necessary lines of C program code. Then you should use a

```
/* To evaluate the difference between two integer numbers */
#include <stdio.h>
main ()
{
/* Description  ..... 
    Evaluate first number minus second number      [cheat001]
    Display the two numbers and the difference      [cheat002]
*/

/* Variables for the two numbers and the difference [cheat003] */


}
```

Figure 2.1

compiler program to convert the program code to a form the computer understands, so that it will be able to run it and, it is hoped, get the required results. If the required results are not obtained, it will be necessary to use the editor program again to make changes to your copy of the exercise file.

If you do not know what code to write for a design statement, you can get help by referring to the contents of the 'cheat' files. These files contain a typical solution. The cheat files are found on the supplied disk in the CHEATS directory. They have names such as `cheat001.C`. These names correspond to the references found at the end of the design statements. In Fig. 2.1. we see a reference for this cheat file at the end of the first design statement. If you have learned how to insert the contents of a file into the file you are working on, you could incorporate the contents of a cheat file directly into your source program file at the appropriate position.

2.4 A first program

The facilities of C that enable us to implement the concepts outlined in Chapter 1 will be gradually introduced during the course. To get started, let us examine a simple program that merely adds two numbers; see Fig. 2.2. When this program is executed, the output on the monitor screen is as follows:

```
First no. is 35 Second no. is 21 Sum is 56
```

Let us now explain this program line by line.

```
/* This program adds two integer numbers */
```

The first line in our program is a comment. A comment is any explanatory text within a program. It must be surrounded by `/*` and `*/`. Comments are ignored by

```
/* This program adds two integer numbers */
#include <stdio.h>
main ()
{
/* Description ......
   Compute the sum of two numbers
   Display the two numbers and the sum
*/
   int   first_number = 35,
         second_number = 21,
         sum ;

   sum = first_number + second_number ;
   printf ("First no. is %d Second no. is %d Sum is %d\n",
      first_number, second_number, sum) ;
}
```

Figure 2.2

the compiler and are included to explain the program to a human reader. They can be placed anywhere in a program. As a matter of style, we will always start our programs with a comment to explain their purpose.

```
#include <stdio.h>
```

This line is an instruction to what is called the *preprocessor* part of the compiler. Its use will be explained in detail later. For the moment we shall consider it as a means by which the compilation system allows us to type input on the keyboard and write output to the monitor screen.

```
main ()
```

All of our programs will include this line (or one very similar) to show where program execution begins. The parentheses indicate to the compiler that main is a function; this concept will be explained in detail later.

```
{
```

Braces enclose the body of a function. They group all of the statements that belong to the function. This brace marks the beginning of such a block of statements.

```
/* Description ......
   Compute the sum of two numbers
   Display the two numbers and the sum
*/
```

Here we have another comment. This time it is spread over a number of lines. As a matter of style and good practice, we will always use comments in this way to explain what the function does and how it does it. Thus we call it the *outline design*.

```
int    first_number = 35,
       second_number = 21,
       sum ;
```

This section of the code is an *integer declaration*. It declares that three variable identifiers first_number, second_number and sum are going to hold integer numbers. We say that int is a C keyword that introduces one or more identifiers. It is followed by the names of the variable identifiers that are option-ally given initial values as for the first two above. There are several different ways to declare variable identifiers and we shall return to this subject later.

```
sum = first_number + second_number ;
```

This line is an *assignment statement*. Read it as 'sum becomes equal to the result of adding first_number to second_number'. It assigns to the variable sum the value of the expression to the right of the equals sign (known as the *assignment operator*). In other words the value contained in the variable first_number is added to the value contained in second_number and the result is stored in the variable sum.

```
printf ("First no. is %d Second no. is %d Sum is %d\n",
    first_number, second_number, sum) ;
```

This is one statement (a function call) spread over two lines. C provides a library of commonly used functions. The function printf writes information to the monitor screen. The details within the parentheses are called *arguments*. In this case there are four, separated by commas. The first argument is enclosed in quotation marks and is called the *control string*. The control string directs or controls the way in which information is displayed. It contains both descriptive text and special control characters. The text, such as First number is, will be displayed on the monitor screen as you see it in the control string. The special control characters, such as %d and \n, are used to position other data to be displayed. The control characters %d indicate that a decimal number is to be displayed. In our case there are going to be three such numbers. The control character \n (newline) indicates that when the last number has been displayed, the screen cursor will be placed at the start of the next line. Arguments two, three and four refer to the program's three variables. Their contents are to be displayed in the order shown.

```
}
```

Finally, the right brace is used to identify the end of the body of function main and in this case the end of the program.

The layout of the program is of little concern to the compiler. Generally, spaces are not significant. For example, the assignment statement in our first example could have been written without any space characters separating the elements of the statement. The use of spaces, comments and blank lines is left to the discretion of the programmer. You will quickly understand that it is possible to produce a program that is readily understood by the compiler but is not so easily read by the human reader. Consequently, throughout this book we use a layout and style that ensure that our programs are easy to follow and read.

The identifiers created by the programmer are a matter of choice, but give an opportunity to describe the data that is to be contained within them. We shall take advantage of this by always using meaningful identifiers. Normally, an identifier will not exceed thirty characters in length. It must start with either a letter or the underscore character _ and its remaining characters may be letters, digits or underscore characters.

Notice that the case used to write C is significant, for example, PRINTF is not the same as printf. If we declare an integer variable as first_number, we cannot then refer to it in an assignment statement by First_Number.

Certain items of punctuation are mandatory parts of the C language. From our first program you will notice that declarations and statements end with a semicolon. This is very important to the compiler; the new programmer generally finds this out quickly. Also, notice that in lists, such as in the list of variable identifiers or the list of arguments of a function, we use a comma to separate components.

One source of error for the new programmer is mismatched symbols that must come in pairs. The comment delimiters /* and */ must be used in pairs. So must { and }, which enclose the body of the function and other sections of a program as we shall see later. Also, ", as used in the control string of a printf argument, must come in pairs.

C contains several keywords such as 'int', each of which has a specific purpose. These keywords must be surrounded by one or more blank characters, and we must not use them as identifiers.

Exercises

1. Tick the valid C identifiers from the following list:

```
velocity      freda      time-of-day    int
tax_rate      x2         4x
```

2. What is the output produced by the following fragment of C source code?

```
first_number = 3 ;
second_number = 5 ;
second_number = first_number ;
printf ("%d %d\n", first_number, second_number) ;
integer_number = 6 ;
integer_number = integer_number + 1 ;
printf ("%d\n", integer_number) ;
```

3. The following program contains syntax errors that the compiler would find. What are they?

```
#include <stdio.h>
main ()
{
    int    anumber
           bnumber
           cnumber ;
/* The program starts here
    anumber := 13
    bnumber = 12
    bnumber = anumber + bnumber ;
    cfigure = bnumber ;
    Printf ("%d %d %d\n, anumber, bnumber, cmunber ;
```

4. Using pencil and paper, finish writing the program whose outline design is given in Fig. 2.3. Check your work, then implement it on the computer as follows:

(i)   Make a copy on your own disk of the exercise outline stored in the file EX0204.C in the EXERCISE directory on the enclosed course disk.

(ii) Use your editor to amend EX0204.C so that it contains your code.

(iii) Compile, run and, if necessary, correct the program.

```
/* To evaluate the difference between two integer numbers */
#include <stdio.h>
main ()
{
/* Description   ......
    Evaluate first number minus second number        [cheat001]
    Display the two numbers and the difference        [cheat002]
*/

/* Variables for the two numbers and the difference [cheat003] */


}
```

Figure 2.3

3

Declarations and assignments for integer numbers

3.1 The concept of data types

A computer program manipulates information, or data, to obtain a desired result. Data is the general expression describing all that is operated on by the computer. In C every item of data is considered to be of a specific type. For example, numbers such as 5 or 23 are examples of integers; in C they are values of the data type int. Whereas 5.2 and 23.69 are examples of real numbers, in C they are values of the data type float.

Different data types are stored and manipulated differently within the machine. Consequently, we must show the type of each identifier at the start of the program. It is a general rule of C that every identifier must be declared before it is used.

3.2 Constant declarations

Some information used in a program never changes, or at least does not change over many executions of the program. Such data are modelled in a program by constants. We often give a symbolic name (or identifier) to a constant so that the name can then be used (instead of the value) throughout the program. Consider the following constant declarations:

```
const int weeks_per_year = 52 ;
const int positive = 1,
          negative = - positive,
          gross = 12 * 12 ;
```

Here we have two constant declarations. The first has one entry such that we can use the identifier weeks_per_year to represent the value 52 throughout our program. The second has a list of three identifiers. Notice how we have used an arithmetic expression, which is evaluated when the program is compiled, for the second and third identifiers in the list. Thus `negative` would have the value of −1 throughout the program and, since `*` is used by C to represent multiplication, `gross` would have the value 144. The keyword `int` denotes that the identifiers following it are of the type integer.

3.3 Variable declarations

Every variable occurring in a program must be declared, or given an identifier, before it is used. Here are some examples:

```
int weekly_pay,
    yearly_pay ;
int total ;
```

We can now imagine some boxes or storage locations within the computer's memory labelled `weekly_pay`, `yearly_pay` and `total` in which we can store integer values. See Fig. 3.1.

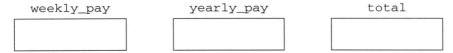

Figure 3.1

3.4 Assignment statements

A value is copied into a variable (placed in the storage location) by means of an assignment statement. In its simplest form an assignment statement consists of a variable identifier, followed by the assignment operator, followed by an expression that will give a value to be placed in the variable. For example,

```
weekly_pay = 400 ;
yearly_pay = 50 * weekly_pay ;
```

would result in new values being given to the storage areas identified by `weekly_pay` and `yearly_pay` as shown in Fig. 3.2.

A program is required to calculate the total salary of an employee over two years. During the second year his weekly pay is increased by £10 and a different

Figure 3.2

```
 ogram to calculate total pay over two years */
 de <stdio.h>
   ()
{
/* Description ......
   Calculate annual pay for first year
   Assign weekly pay rate for second year
   Calculate annual pay for second year
   Calculate and display the sum of the salaries for the two years
*/
   const int weeks_per_year = 52,
             low_bonus_factor = 1,
             high_bonus_factor = 2 ;

   int weekly_pay = 50,
       first_year_pay,
       second_year_pay,
       total_pay ;

   first_year_pay = weekly_pay * low_bonus_factor *
      weeks_per_year ;
   weekly_pay = weekly_pay + 10 ;
   second_year_pay = weekly_pay * high_bonus_factor *
      weeks_per_year ;
   total_pay = first_year_pay + second_year_pay ;
   printf ("First is %d Second is %d Total is %d\n",
      first_year_pay, second_year_pay, total_pay) ;
}
```

Figure 3.3

bonus factor is used. This program, given in Fig. 3.3, illustrates the use of constant declarations, variable declarations and assignment statements.

You will notice several statements that are similar to those found in our first example program in the previous chapter. We will explain the program beginning at the constant declaration.

```
const int weeks_per_year = 52,
          low_bonus_factor = 1,
          high_bonus_factor = 2 ;
```

We have three integer constants declared here introduced by the keyword `const` and followed by the data type `int`. The constant identifiers and their associated constant values are separated by commas. Note that we could have declared the three constants in two or three separate constant declarations one after the other. For example,

```
const int weeks_per_year = 52 ;
const int low_bonus_factor = 1 ;
const int high_bonus_factor = 2 ;
```

In this case, each constant identifier is preceded by const and int and each declaration is terminated by a semicolon.

Next we have the variable declaration, a list of four integer variable identifiers:

```
int weekly_pay = 50,
    first_year_pay,
    second_year_pay,
    total_pay ;
```

Note that the first variable, weekly_pay, has been given an initial value. It must be stressed that this is not the same as a constant. The value of a constant may *not* be changed during the execution of a program, but a variable given an initial value may have its value changed any time during execution. We have chosen to declare all four identifiers in one declaration. We could have declared them using two, three or four separate declarations. For example,

```
int weekly_pay = 50 ;
int first_year_pay ;
int second_year_pay ;
int total_pay ;
```

Now we have each identifier preceded by int and each declaration terminated by a semicolon.

The first four executable statements of this program are assignment statements:

```
first_year_pay = weekly_pay * low_bonus_factor *
    weeks_per_year ;
weekly_pay = weekly_pay + 10 ;
second_year_pay = weekly_pay * high_bonus_factor *
    weeks_per_year ;
total_pay = first_year_pay + second_year_pay ;
```

We should read the first one as 'first_year_pay becomes equal to the result given when weekly_pay is multiplied by low_bonus_factor multiplied by weeks_per_year'. In effect, the expression on the right hand side of the equals sign is evaluated and the resulting value is stored in first_year_pay.

The second assignment statement illustrates that when the value of an expression is assigned to a variable, that variable loses any previous value and takes the new value. In this case, the value of weekly_pay before execution of this statement is 50 (it was initialized to this value when it was declared); after execution the value will be 60. Another way of achieving the same result for this statement is by using a different assignment operator.

```
weekly_pay += 10 ;
```

Using the += assignment operator gives us a shorthand form that adds 10 to the value of weekly_pay.

Finally, we display the results on the screen:

Statement number	weekly_pay	first_year_pay	second_year_pay	total_pay
declaration	50			
1		2600		
2	60			
3			6240	
4				8840

Figure 3.4

```
printf ("First is %d Second is %d Total is %d\n",
    first_year_pay, second_year_pay, total_pay) ;
```

The `printf` function will display the text and the values held in the three integer variables in the order given before moving the cursor to the start of the next line on the monitor screen. Recall that the first argument of the function, the control string, determines the way in which the information is to be displayed. Hence the output on the monitor screen is:

```
First is 2600 Second is 6240 Total is 8840
```

We can illustrate the way in which this program is executed by using a *trace table*, sometimes called a *dry run table*. Fig. 3.4 is a trace table of the execution of the program we have just described. In it we have given numbers to the executable statements.

Taking each statement step by step allows us to see the results after execution of each statement and finally allows us to read off the values that would be displayed by the `printf` statement. Tracing the execution of a program in this way is a useful technique for finding logical errors in the code.

The basic assignment operator is the equals sign. This is what we have used in our programs so far, giving the general form of assignment statement:

```
variable = expression ;
```

C provides several variations to this to allow for commonly used situations. The general form of these variations is:

```
variable  operation= expression ;
```

where operation may be any of the four basic arithmetic operators and is equivalent to:

```
variable = variable operation expression ;
```

Here are some examples followed by the equivalent code using the equals assignment operator:

```
wages += 1000 ;
wages = wages + 1000 ;                                          (3-1)

pay -= taxable_pay * tax_rate ;
pay = pay - taxable_pay * tax_rate  ;                           (3-2)

sum_of_money *= investment + 20 ;
sum_of_money = sum_of_money * (investment + 20) ;     (3-3)
```

Notice that in example (3-3) we have put parentheses around the expression. This is to show that the addition is done first before the multiplication. Parentheses were not needed in example (3-2), because the multiplication is automatically done first before the subtraction. The reasons for this are to do with the order in which arithmetic operators are evaluated, as we see in the next section.

3.5   The data type integer

A value of type integer is a whole number lying within limits defined by our compiler system. The minimum and maximum integer values for a C system are defined by the constants INT_MIN and INT_MAX. So far we have seen variables and constants of type int that allow for values in the range INT_MIN = -32768 to INT_MAX = 32767 on some C systems. The values of all integer variables, integer constants and intermediate integer arithmetic results must lie within these limits. If they do not, the results may not be correct, giving a condition known as *underflow* or *overflow*.

If a larger range is required, then one can use the type long int (or just long for short), which typically has a range of LONG_MIN = -2147483648 to LONG_MAX = 2147483647. Other integer types are also available.

The following arithmetic operators are used in integer expressions and give an integer value when applied to integer operands:

Operator	Meaning
*	to multiply
/	to divide
%	to give remainder after division
+	to add
-	to subtract or negate
++	to increase by 1
--	to decrease by 1

Integer division produces a truncated result (not rounded up or down).   For example,

```
sales_value = 23 / 5 ;
```

would assign the value 4 to sales_value as 5 goes into 23 four whole times.

The % operator gives the remainder after division. For example,

```
left_over = 23 % 5 ;
```

would assign the value 3 to left_over.

The operators + and − may be used as unary operators. That is, each can be placed in front of an operand without another operand preceding it, as in the following statements:

```
number1 = − 2 * 4 * number2 * number3 ;
number2 = + 5 * number3 / number4 ;
```

In the above examples then, the unary operator − changes the sign of the operand following it; however, the unary operator + leaves the sign of the operator following it unchanged.

The ++ and −− operators allow a shorthand for increasing and decreasing by one. They are used as in the following statements that are followed by equivalent code using + and − .

```
++ counter ;
counter = counter + 1 ;                                    (3-4)

−− exam_mark ;
exam_mark = exam_mark − 1 ;                                 (3-5)

total = ++ sum ;
total = sum + 1 ;                                          (3-6)

result = 7 * −− number ;
result = 7 * (number − 1) ;                                (3-7)
```

Note that in (3-4) and (3-5) we have changed the value of the variable by +1 and −1 respectively. In (3-6) and (3-7) we have used the shorthand within an arithmetic expression.

When an arithmetic expression is evaluated, the normal priorities (precedence) of the above operators apply:

Any expression in parentheses is evaluated first, then
++, −−, unary + and unary − have priority over
*, / and %, which have priority over
+ and −.

When two operators of the same priority are contained within an expression (for example, a * b / c), evaluation is from left to right. Let us now consider some integer expressions, paying particular attention to the operator precedence.

```
5 * 5 / 2                                                 (3-8)

5 * (5 / 2)                                               (3-9)
```

In (3-8), the result is 12 (5 * 5 = 25, 25 / 2 = 12), whereas (3-9) results in 10, (5 / 2 = 2, 5 * 2 = 10).

```
2 * 3 + 4                                                           (3-10)

5 + 3 * 4                                                           (3-11)
```

In (3-10), the multiplication is done first, so we have 2 * 3 = 6, then 6 + 4, giving 10. In (3-11), again the multiplication is done first. This time we have 5 +12, giving 17.

```
(a + b)c                                                            (3-12)

3 * (a + b)                                                         (3-13)

2 * 3 - 4 * 5                                                       (3-14)
```

The expression in (3-12) is not valid because an implied multiplication is used. We cannot imply operators as we may in mathematics. We would have to write (a + b) * c. In (3-13), the term in parentheses is evaluated first, then its result is multiplied by 3. This is the way to write the C statement for the mathematical expression $3(a + b)$. In (3-14), the multiplications are evaluated first, then their products are subtracted. So we have 6 – 20, giving –14.

```
13 / 5                                                             (3-15)

13 % 5                                                             (3-16)
```

In (3-15), we note that integer division gives a truncated result, so we get a result of 2. In (3-16), we note that the % operator gives the remainder after division, so we get a result of 3.

```
(4 + 9) / 2 * 3                                                   (3-17)

(4 + 9) / (2 * 3)                                                 (3-18)
```

In (3-17), the term in parentheses is evaluated, then the terms are evaluated from left to right. Hence 13 divided by 2 gives 6, which is then multiplied by 3 to give a final result of 18. In (3-18) both terms in parentheses are evaluated, hence 13 divided by 6 gives a result of 2.

Notice that the spaces separating the operators are optional, but included to aid readability. For example, (3-10) above might have been written 2*3+4.

3.6   Integer output

As we have seen, the printf function will display our output on the monitor screen. The way it controls the format of the output is by the control string (also called the *format string*). We now examine this in more detail so that we can have more control over the way in which we present our output.

The place where a value is displayed is called its *field* and the number of character positions it occupies including any leading spaces is called its *field width*. Consider the printf statement

```
printf ("%d%d%d\n", rate1, rate2, total) ;
```

This would output the values of `rate1`, `rate2` and `total` using a field width that is equivalent to the number of digits in each value. For example, if `rate1`, `rate2` and `total` contained the values 9800, 240 and 10040 respectively, the output would be

```
980024010040
```

We can improve on that by simply inserting a space between each of the format specifiers (`%d`). Hence,

```
printf ("%d %d %d\n", rate1, rate2, total) ;
```

would give an output of

```
9800 240 10040
```

But what if we wished to tabulate our output so that columns of figures are aligned? In such cases we specify a field width to be used for each argument. For example,

```
printf ("%6d%6d%6d\n", rate1, rate2, total) ;
```

would give an output of

```
  9800   240 10040
```

that is, with each value occupying 6 positions justified to the right of a 6-character field.

If we make the field width too small for the value to be printed, then the field width will automatically be increased just enough to fit the value. As we have seen, omitting the field width gives an implied field width of the number of digits in the value used.

If we are using `long` integers we have to modify our format specifiers. Instead of using `%d` we would use `%ld` (that is, % followed by the letter l, then d). For example,

```
printf ("%ld %d\n", large_number, small_number) ;
```

would be necessary if `large_number` had been declared as of type `long int`.

Study the program given in Fig. 3.5 and note the positions of the results. The output on two lines is:

```
671457     123  -987
671457 123 -987
```

Note that there are 4 spaces between `671457` and `123` on the first line, because in addition to the field width of 6 for `little`, there is a space between `%ld` and `%6d` in the control string.

```
/* To illustrate integer output options */
#include <stdio.h>
main ()
{
/* Description ......
   Assign initial values to the variables
   Display results with different field widths
*/
   long int large ;
   int      little,
            negative_one ;

   large = 671457 ;
   little = 123 ;
   negative_one = -987 ;
   printf ("%ld %6d %5d\n", large, little, negative_one) ;
   printf ("%3ld %2d %3d\n", large, little, negative_one) ;
}
```

Figure 3.5

Exercises

1. Give the result of the following integer expressions (where possible):
   (i)   27 / 8
   (ii)   27 % 5
   (iii) − 27 * 3
   (iv)   − 27 * 3 + 4
   (v)   2 * 17 / (3 + 2) % 4
   (vi)   3 (2 − 9)
   (vii) 5 * ++ 3 / 4
2. Draw a trace table for the program given in Fig. 3.6. What is the resultant output?
3. Finish writing the program whose outline design is given in Fig. 3.7. The program should assign the value 1234 to the variable field_one and then assign the result of field_one minus 6757 to the variable field_two. The two variables should then be displayed, without any text, as follows:
   (i) without specifying field widths; then
   (ii) with a field width of 6 for both variables; then
   (iii) with a field width of 4 for both variables.
       When you have completed this task, use your editor to insert your lines of code into your copy of the file EX0303.C. When this is done you should check your program and attempt to compile and run it. Check that the results you have achieved are the same as you expected to get.
4. Finish writing the program whose outline design is given in Fig. 3.8.

The program is to calculate the minimum number of coins (10p, 5p, 1p) needed to pay out a particular sum of money held in a variable called sum_of_money. This variable should be given an initial value in pence. For example, a sum of 37 pence would require three 10p coins, one 5p coin and two 1p coins.

When you have completed this task, use the editor to insert your lines of code into your copy of the file EX0304.C. When this is done, you should check your program and attempt to compile and run the program.

```
/* Illustrates various assignment statements */
#include <stdio.h>
main()
{
/* Description  ......
   Make assignments
   Display results
*/
   const int five = 5,
             minus2 = - 2 ;

   int   varone,
         vartwo ;

   varone = 9 - 3 * 2 ;
   vartwo = (minus2 * varone) * - 1 ;
   vartwo = 2 * vartwo + 1 ;
   varone = vartwo * vartwo - 41 ;
   vartwo += 20 ;
   varone = (varone - 2) * (varone - 2) ;
   printf ("%d %d %d %d\n", five, minus2, varone, vartwo) ;
}
```

Figure 3.6

```
/* A program to experiment with field widths */
#include <stdio.h>
main()
{
/* Description  ......
   Make initial assignments                  [cheat006]
   Display results with no field widths       [cheat007]
   Display results with field width of 6      [cheat008]
   Display results with field width of 4      [cheat009]
*/

/* Declare all necessary variables            [cheat010] */


}
```

Figure 3.7

```
/* Calculates minimum number of coins for a sum of money */
#include <stdio.h>
main ()
{
/* Description ......
    Calculate number of 10p coins and amount left over     [cheat011]
    Calculate number of 5p coins and 1p coins              [cheat012]
    Display results                                        [cheat013]
*/

/* variables for sum of money, the numbers of 10p, 5p and 1p    */
/* coins required and the amount left over after the number of */
/* 10p coins has been calculated                  [cheat014] */


}
```

Figure 3.8

4

Real numbers

4.1 The data type `float`

A value of type `float` is an element of a system-defined subset of real numbers, such as 23.75 or 0.5.

As with integers we can define constant identifiers of type `float`:

```
const float discount = 41.2,
             percentage = 0.75 ;
const float overtime_rate = 1.5 ;
```

We can also declare variables of type `float`:

```
float unit_cost,
      total_cost ;
```

Floating constants are written with a decimal point. They can be written in a fixed-point form (decimal notation), in which case there is normally at least one digit on each side of the decimal point, for example, 32.5, 0.075. Also, they may be written using an exponentiation notation (also called scientific notation), for example, 1.5426e5, where e5 means multiply 1.5426 by 10 to the power of 5. For the sake of simplicity, we shall always use the more familiar fixed-point form in the examples and exercises that follow.

Each C system defines limits on the range (the smallest and largest allowable values) and precision (maximum number of significant digits) of floating numbers. An attempt to evaluate a value outside the given range results in overflow or underflow. Limited precision can give rise to inaccuracies; for example, on a computer working to seven significant figures 1000.0 + 0.0001 would give 1000.000.

Computers use base 2, that is, they use the binary digits of 0 and 1 to represent numbers. Many real numbers, such as 0.9, can be expressed exactly as a decimal using base 10, but cannot be expressed exactly in base 2. This means that the number actually stored within the machine and used in calculations could be an approximation of the true value.

The maximum and minimum `float` values for a C system are defined by system constants `FLT_MIN` and `FLT_MAX`. If a larger range of real numbers is needed, we can use the type `double` that will allow for very large or very small numbers.

4.2 Real expressions

We call expressions that manipulate values of type `float` *real expressions*. We use the same basic operators in real expressions that we have already seen in integer expressions, except for the `%` operator, which obviously has an application only with integers.

C allows you to mix integers and real numbers in arithmetic expressions. Each time `operand_1 operator operand_2` is evaluated in an expression, the value produced will be of type `int` if both `operand_1` and `operand_2` are integers, and of type `float` if one or both of the operands is a real number. This can be illustrated by the following:

```
7 / 4
```
(4-1)

```
7.0 / 4
```
(4-2)

```
7 / 4.0
```
(4-3)

```
7.0 / 4.0
```
(4-4)

The result of (4-1) is 1, but (4-2), (4-3) and (4-4) all give a result of 1.75.

When you assign the value of an expression to a variable you must ensure that their types are compatible. You may assign an integer expression to a real (`float`) variable, the resulting integer value (4, say) is converted to the corresponding real number (4.0 in this case). However, you cannot assign a real expression to an integer (`int`) variable.

Let us consider some examples of assignment statements that use real expressions and mixed expressions. We will assume that in each case the identifier `result` is of type `float` and the identifier `number` is of type `int` with an initial value of 3.

```
result = (2.1 + number) / (2 * 5) ;
```

This will give a result of 0.51. The terms in parentheses give 5.1 (`float`) and 10 (`int`) respectively.

```
result = (2.0 + number) / 2 * 5 ;
```

The expression in parentheses gives 5.0 (`float`), this is divided by 2 to give 2.5 (`float`) and then multiplied by 5 to give 12.5.

```
result = (2 + number) / 2 * 5 ;
```

The expression in parentheses gives 5 (int); this is divided by 2 to give 2 (int) and then multiplied by 5 to give the result 10 (int), which is then assigned to the float variable result as 10.0.

```
result = (12.0 + number) / (2 * 5) ;
```

The expressions in parentheses give 15.0 (float) and 10 (int) respectively. The first expression divided by the second gives the result 1.5 (float) that is assigned to the float variable result.

```
result = (12 + number) / (2 * 5) ;
```

The terms in parentheses give 15 (integer) and 10 (integer). The first expression divided by the second gives the result 1 (integer), which is assigned to the float variable result as 1.0.

```
result = number / 2 ;
```

This gives a result of 1 (int), because both operands of the expression are of type int, which is assigned to the float variable result as 1.0. If we wish to allow for the fractional part in the result then we must make at least one of the operands of type float. For example,

```
result = number / 2.0 ;
```

will give a result of 1.5. Alternatively, we can make the compiler reinterpret the type of a variable in an expression by preceding it with another type in parentheses. So, we might write

```
result = (float) number / 2 ;
```

which also gives a result of 1.5.

4.3   Output of real values

We have seen that when displaying integers, we may specify a field width (for example, using %6d). If the field width was specified too small or not at all, the default width used by C would be just big enough to fit the value. When we use printf to output values of type float, we must again use appropriate format specifications in the control string. We can output the value of a float variable by specifying both the field width and the number of decimal places, or use default values. For example a value displayed with a field width of 9 and with 3 decimal places would occupy 9 positions, 5 for the integer part, 1 for the decimal point and 3 for the fractional part:

```
12345.123
```

The first example below illustrates how to specify both the field width and the number of decimal places. The remaining examples illustrate what happens when one or both are omitted:

```
printf ("Results: %6.2f %6.2f\n", result1, result2) ;
```

would output the contents of the float variables in fields of width 6 and with 2 places of decimals with a space between the two fields generated by the space in the control string. With the values of 34.5 and 35, we would have:

```
Results:   34.50   35.00
```

This allows for tabular output and is realistic in the precision of the results.

```
printf ("Results: %.2f %.2f\n", result1, result2) ;
```

would output the contents of the float variables to two decimal places using field widths sufficient to hold all the significant digits and with a space between the two fields. Therefore, with values of 0.5 and 3.75 we would have:

```
Results: 0.50 3.75
```

This is ideal for non-tabular results with realistic precision.

```
printf ("Results: %10f %10f\n", result1, result2) ;
```

would output the contents of the float variables result1 and result2 in fields of width 10 with a default value of 6 for the number of decimal places, each with a space between the two fields. Therefore with values of 34.5 and 35 we would have:

```
Results:   34.500000   35.000000
```

This allows for tabular output, but is extravagant in terms of the accuracy of the results. Notice that zeros are displayed.

```
printf ("Output is: %f\n", result) ;
```

would output the contents of the float variable result as a fixed point number to 6 places of decimals (the default in C) and a field width just large enough to hold the value. If result held 34.5, the output would be:

```
Output is: 34.500000
```

Let us now consider the sample program given by Fig. 4.1. The output from this program would be:

```
Pendulum length: 213.60 cms. Period 2.93 secs.
```

In this program we find some statements and ideas that are introduced in this chapter. We will discuss these.

```
#include <stdio.h>
#include <math.h>
```

```
/* A program to calculate the period of a pendulum */
#include <stdio.h>
#include <math.h>
main ()
{
/* Description  ......
   Assign value to pendulum length
   Calculate the period
   Display length and period in fixed point format
*/
   const float pi = 3.14159265,
               gravity = 981 ;   /* acceleration due to gravity */

   float pendulum_length,        /* length of pendulum in cms. */
         period ;                /* period in seconds */

   pendulum_length = 213.6 ;
   period = 2 * pi * sqrt (pendulum_length / gravity) ;
   printf ("Pendulum length: %.2f cms. Period %.2f secs.\n",
      pendulum_length, period) ;
}
```

Figure 4.1

We are familiar by now with the #include statement for stdio.h. The new statement allows us to use certain mathematical functions, in our case the square root function.

```
const float pi = 3.14159265,
            gravity = 981 ;
```

Here we have a constant declaration of two float constants introduced by the keywords const and float.

```
float pendulum_length,
      period ;
```

Now we have a list of two variables of type float.

```
pendulum_length = 213.6 ;
```

This is a simple assignment of a float value to the float variable.

```
period = 2 * pi * sqrt (pendulum_length / gravity) ;
```

This is a well-known formula that has been translated into a C assignment statement incorporating a real expression. The expression would be evaluated in the following manner. The term in parentheses is calculated first. The square root of this is calculated next. The period is then calculated by multiplying 2 by the constant value for π and then multiplying this intermediate result by the result from the sqrt function.

Exercises

1. Assuming that a, b, and c have been assigned real values, write a C assignment statement to evaluate the following:

$$\frac{2a + 4c}{3b}$$

2. Show the output obtained from:

```
printf ("%9.3f %2.2f\n", 41.57, 79.341) ;
printf ("%f %.4f\n", 325.7, 0.00472) ;
```

3. A program is required to calculate and display an employee's gross and net pay. Gross pay is given by: basic pay + overtime rate * overtime hours. Tax is deducted from the gross pay at the current rate of 25% to obtain the net pay. The tax rate (.25), an overtime rate (10.50) and the normal working week of 40 hours should be defined as constants. Basic pay and the total hours worked should be assigned values of 227.50 and 44.5 respectively.

   Finish coding the program whose outline design is given as Fig. 4.2. When you have completed this, use the editor to insert lines of code into your copy of the file EX0403.C, check it and then compile and run the program.

4. The annual mortgage repayment (R) is given by

$$R = \frac{Ar\left(1 + \dfrac{r}{100}\right)^n}{\left\{100\left[\left(1 + \dfrac{r}{100}\right)^n - 1\right]\right\}}$$

   where A = amount borrowed

   n = term of the mortgage (years)

   r = interest rate (%)

   Complete the program to calculate R. The outline design is given in Fig. 4.3. The interest rate should be defined as a constant; the amount borrowed and term should be assigned values. When you have completed the program, use the editor in the usual way to insert lines of code into your copy of the file EX0404.C, check it and then compile and run the program.

   The program will need to use the function pow to raise an expression to some power and therefore will need to include math.h. The function pow takes two arguments: the first is the expression and the second the power. For example, to raise alpha * beta to the power 3, we would write

```
pow (alpha * beta, 3)
```

   Use the data: 12.0 for interest rate, 22000 for amount borrowed, and 25 for the term of the mortgage. What is the expected result?

```
/* Calculates gross pay and net pay after tax */
#include <stdio.h>
main ()
{
/* Description  ......
   Initialize basic pay and total hours worked      [cheat016]
   Calculate gross pay and net pay                  [cheat017]
   Display results                                  [cheat018]
*/

/* Define tax rate, overtime rate and normal hours  [cheat019] */

/* Declare variables for gross pay, net pay,                  */
/* basic pay and total hours worked                [cheat020] */

}
```

Figure 4.2

```
/* Calculates annual mortgage repayment */
#include <stdio.h>
#include <math.h>
main ()
{
/* Description  ......
   Assign values to amount borrowed and term  [cheat021]
   Calculate and display the yearly repayment [cheat022]
*/

/* Define the interest rate                    [cheat023] */

/* Declare all the variables                   [cheat024] */


}
```

Figure 4.3

5

Input and output

5.1 Introduction

The pendulum program, as written in the previous chapter, has only limited use in that it will evaluate the period for the same pendulum length every time the program is executed. One of the main reasons for writing a program is that we write it once and then run it several times, often with different data values at each run. To achieve this with the pendulum program as it stands, we would have to change the statement assigning a value to the length before each run. It would be better if the value of `pendulum_length` is supplied to the program by an external device at each run. This would allow us to change `pendulum_length` (that is, the input data) at each run, without changing the program.

Another reason for separating the data and the program is that the program may be processing a large amount of data that should not use valuable space in main memory as part of the program.

Obviously, results from a program must be recorded. We have already seen that this can be done on the monitor screen. Sometimes it is more convenient to store the information in a computer file.

Since computer output is often read by people who have not seen the program, it is essential that the output should be self-explanatory with appropriate headings, captions and so forth. As we have already seen, we achieve this by writing explanatory text with the results.

The purpose of this chapter is fourfold:

1. To show how we enhance output data to a monitor screen using the function `printf`.
2. To show how we can input data from a keyboard using the function `scanf`.
3. To indicate the input and output requirements of an interactive program.
4. To demonstrate how to use data files.

5.2   Writing to the monitor screen

The standard function `printf` can be used in a variety of ways to produce output on the monitor screen. We will now illustrate some of the facilities it provides to enhance the way in which we display the results of our programs.

Assume that the integer variables `value1`, `value2`, `value3`, `value4`, `value5` have values of 1, 2, 3, 4, 5 respectively.

```
printf ("%6d", value1) ;
printf ("%6d", value2) ;
printf ("%6d", value3) ;
printf ("%6d", value4) ;
```

can be written as:

```
printf ("%6d%6d%6d%6d", value1, value2, value3,
    value4) ;
```

Both would write the following to the monitor screen:

```
1     2     3     4
```

It is useful to think of a pointer that moves along the output line and shows the position for the next value. To move this pointer on to the next line, we use

```
printf ("%6d%6d%6d%6d\n", value1, value2, value3,
    value4) ;
```

This writes `value1` to `value4` and then terminates the current line by sending an end-of-line marker (\n) to the monitor screen. Subsequent output will be on the next line. For example,

```
printf ("%6d%6d\n", value1, value2) ;
printf ("%6d%6d", value3, value4) ;
printf ("\n") ;
printf ("%6d\n", value5) ;
```

is equivalent to

```
printf ("%6d%6d\n", value1, value2) ;
printf ("%6d%6d\n", value3, value4) ;
printf ("%6d\n", value5) ;
```

Both would produce the following on the monitor screen:

```
1     2
3     4
5
```

The control character \n can also be used at the beginning of the control string.

For example, to obtain a blank line

```
printf ("%6d%6d\n\n", value1, value2) ;
printf ("%6d%6d%6d\n", value3, value4, value5) ;
```

is equivalent to

```
printf ("%6d%6d\n", value1, value2) ;
printf ("\n%6d%6d%6d\n", value3, value4, value5) ;
```

Both would produce

```
1     2
                (a blank line)
3     4     5
```

There may be any number of arguments to printf. The first is always a control string enclosed in double quotes. After that, the arguments may be variables, constants or expressions. It is most important that the number of conversion (or format) specifications in the control string matches the number of arguments following the control string.

The conversion specifications we have seen so far are %d and %f. With %d we have seen that we may need to use a field width qualifier, such as in %6d to show a field width of six. With %f we have seen that we may need to use either or both the field width qualifier or precision (number of decimal places), such as in %8.2f to show a minimum total field width of eight and two decimal places. The major advantage of using these qualifiers is in tabulating our output. If we produce many numbers on several lines they could be aligned on the right-hand side of the field underneath each other, and real numbers could have their decimal points aligned.

We have also seen that the control string may contain text such as in

```
printf ("The result is %d cms.\n", width) ;
```

The effect of executing this statement is that every character within the quotation marks is sent to the monitor screen, except that %d is replaced by the contents of the variable width. Notice that all spaces within the control string are significant; there will be a space before the width and one after it.

Another way of achieving the same result is to use the character string conversion specification %s. For example,

```
printf ("%s%d%s\n", "The result is ", width, " cms.") ;
```

Here we have a control string that expects a character string followed by an integer variable followed by another string. The character strings are specified in quotation marks as further arguments to the function. We shall return to the subject of character strings later.

5.3   Reading from the keyboard

To read data from the keyboard we use the standard function `scanf`. Like `printf`, this function takes a control string as its first argument. Subsequent arguments allow data to be placed in variables. Let us consider some examples of the use of `scanf`. Assume that we have declared `value1` and `value2` as variables of type `int`, and `realnum1`, and `realnum2` as variables of type `float`. We may use `scanf` as follows:

```
scanf ("%d", &value1) ;
```

This will cause the next value that is typed at the keyboard to be interpreted as an integer and stored in the variable `value1`. Notice that we have a control string with a conversion specification of `%d` to indicate integer. Also, we have not just written the name of the variable into which we want a value placed, but have preceded it by `&`. There is a technical reason for this. For the time being, please simply take on trust that it is important to precede variables used as arguments in a `scanf` function with a `&`.

If we wish, we may use `scanf` to input several values, for example

```
scanf ("%d%f%f%d", &value1, &realnum1, &realnum2,
    &value2) ;
```

Notice that for each value to be read we have a conversion specification, and each variable is preceded by `&`.

The input would be typed in at the keyboard with at least one space between each value and then the <ENTER> key would be pressed. For example,

```
1 7.8 3.4 2<Enter>
```

would cause 1 to be stored in `value1`, 7.8 to be stored in `realnum1`, 3.4 in `realnum2` and 2 in `value2`. It is helpful to think of a pointer moving along the input values as they are assigned to the variables. Alternatively, the input might be typed on two, three or even four lines. In such cases the pointer will automatically move to a new line (if necessary) to obtain the four numeric values required by the `scanf` statement.

5.4   Interactive input and output

When typing data at the keyboard, the user is interacting with the program while it is running. Consider a program containing:

```
scanf ("%d%d", &value1, &value2) ;
```

At this point, it would stop and wait for the user to type in two values. Once they have been typed in and the <ENTER> key pressed, the values would be assigned to `value1` and `value2`, and the program would continue.

But there is a problem. How does the user know that the program has stopped and is waiting for the values? The program should prompt the user to type the required values. Consider the following example:

```
printf ("Please input two values ") ;
scanf ("%d%d", &value1, &value2) ;
```

The character string requesting the user to type in the values would be displayed on the monitor screen. The program would then stop at the scanf function. The user, having been prompted, would type in the values, press the <ENTER> key and the program would then continue.

This is a small example of interactive input and output. In it, we have observed the need for a prompt for the interactive user. Also, we must be aware that the output from an interactive program should be minimal (the user does not want to watch the program writing long, predictable messages). In particular an interactive program should not copy data from input to output, because the user can see his own input. Ideally, an interactive program should report immediately to the user if the input value is not acceptable for processing and give some indication of what is expected.

Let us now consider the short interactive program given as Fig. 5.1 (p.36). If we were to run this program we would have the following dialogue on the screen:

```
Please type a number 1.3
This number squared is :     1.690
Please type another number 2.5
This number cubed is :   15.625
```

Having typed in the required value(s) the user must press the <ENTER> key. This enables the program to continue and means that the next printf statement will output on a new line.

5.5   Using data files

Instead of typing data at the keyboard, we can store information in files in our own disk areas and use the data as input to our programs. Also, instead of writing our results directly to a monitor screen, we may write information to a data file that could be printed later or used as input to another program.

When creating data files to be used as input to a program (for example, by using an editor), we have to specify a file name according to the conventions of the computer's operating system. Similarly, when we write to a data file from within a program we must specify the name of the file to be created and written to.

To specify the input and output files used by a program, we declare special identifiers called file pointers. For example,

```
FILE *my_input_file ;
FILE *my_output_file ;
```

```
/* Illustrates the use of interactive input/output */
#include <stdio.h>
#include <math.h>
main ()
{
/* Description  ......
   Prompt for the first number and read it
   Output square of the first number
   Prompt for second number and read it
   Compute and output the cube
*/
   float first_number,
         second_number,
         second_number_cubed ;

   printf ("Please type a number ") ;
   scanf ("%f", &first_number) ;
   printf ("This number squared is : %7.3f\n",
      pow (first_number, 2)) ;
   printf ("Please type another number ") ;
   scanf ("%f", &second_number) ;
   second_number_cubed = pow (second_number, 3) ;
   printf ("This number cubed is : %7.3f\n",
      second_number_cubed) ;
}
```

Figure 5.1

declares the file pointers my_input_file and my_output_file. Notice that
the type is FILE and should always be written using capital letters. The identifier
that follows is always preceded by * to indicate that it is a *pointer*. Within the
program we always use the file pointer to refer to a particular file.

To associate the file pointer with the file name as used by the operating system,
we use the fopen function. If we wanted to read from the file called
myinput.txt and write to a new file to be called myresult.txt, we would
write the following:

```
my_input_file = fopen ("myinput.txt", "r") ;
my_output_file = fopen ("myresult.txt", "w") ;
```

We observe that the fopen function has two arguments. The first is a character
string constant containing the name of the file as known to the operating system.
Great care should be taken when writing or typing this name. If an error is present
in an input file name, the program will behave incorrectly. Indeed, if a program
does not work correctly, this should be one of the first things to be checked. The
second argument is also a string constant known as the *mode*. The mode may be
"r" to show that the file is to be read, "w" to create a file for writing, or some
others that we will not explore here.

The fopen function is normally placed at the beginning of the executable part of the program. Also, for convenience, it may be combined with the declaration of the file pointer.

```
FILE *my_input_file = fopen ("myinput.txt", "r") ;
FILE *my_output_file = fopen ("myresult.txt", "w") ;
```

To read from or write to our data files, we use the standard functions fscanf and fprintf. These can be used in the same way as scanf and printf, except that, because we may have many files in a single program, it is necessary to specify which file is being read from or written to. The first argument of the fscanf and fprintf functions is the file pointer. For example:

```
fscanf (my_input_file, "%d%d", &value1, &value2) ;
```

reads the next two numbers from the file myinput.txt and assigns them to the variables value1 and value2.

```
fprintf (my_output_file, "Results are: %d\n", total) ;
```

specifies that the text and contents of the variable total are to be output with a following new line symbol to the file myresult.txt.

When we are finished with the files, we must close them with the fclose function. For example,

```
fclose (my_input_file) ;
fclose (my_output_file) ;
```

Now examine the program given as Fig. 5.2, in particular the input and output statements to see where and how they are used.

Exercises

1. Refer to the program in Fig. 5.1 and the resulting screen dialogue, then answer the following questions.
   (i) At which lines did the program stop and wait for input?
   (ii) Which lines contain a prompt?
   (iii) What values have been input by the user?
   (iv) Why is there a space between number and 1.3 on the screen?
   (v) What would the screen dialogue look like if the first printf had a \n at the end of the control string?
2. Refer to the program in Fig. 5.2 and answer the following questions.
   (i) Which identifiers are file pointers?
   (ii) How can you distinguish between an input file and an output file?
   (iii) What is the difference between bhinp and bhinp.dat?
   (iv) Why do we have to specify the file pointer identifier as a parameter of fscanf or fprintf?
   (v) Why might it be a good idea to write the input data to the output file?

(vi)   How would you check that the results of the program are correct?

(vii) How would you produce an input file for the program?

3. Complete the interactive program whose outline is given as Fig. 5.3. The program is to accept input from the keyboard of the x and y coordinates of two points, and output the distance between the two points with suitable text on the screen. (The distance between two points is defined as the square root of $(x_1-x_2)^2 + (y_1-y_2)^2$ where (x_1, y_1) is the first point and (x_2, y_2) is the second.)

When you have completed this task, you should use the editor in the normal way to insert your lines of code into your copy of the file EX0503.C. When this is done you should check it and then attempt to compile and run the program. Run the program several times with different data. To help you, the coordinates (0, 3) and (4, 0) give a result of 5.0.

4. Complete the program whose outline design is given as Fig. 5.4. The program reads three integers representing a date (day, month, year) from the data file EX0504.DAT, and writes the date without spaces in the form day/month/year, writing only the last two digits of the year (93 for 1993, 12 for 1812 and so on). Your output should be written to a file using appropriate text and a format similar to that given in the example program shown in Fig. 5.2.

The outline program is found in the file EX0504.C. You should edit your copy of this file to insert your lines of code. When this is done, you should compile and run the program.

This is the first exercise to use files. you will need to copy the input file EX0504.DAT from the EXERCISE directory of the supplied disk on to your own disk. Failure to ensure that the data file is available to the program will result in the program behaving incorrectly. Results from the program will not appear on the screen, but should be found in the output file that you have specified in the program.

5. The file EX0505.DAT contains two integer numbers. The first number is the length of a garden in metres and the second is the length of a small piece of fencing in centimetres. Complete the program whose outline is shown as Fig. 5.5. The program reads the two integers and calculates how many whole fence pieces are required and the waste (in centimetres) that must be cut off the last piece of fencing. Your output file should include headings, end-titles, suitable text and the input data, that is, a layout similar to that of the previous question. You may assume that the last fence will need cutting and that both input values are not greater than 100. The outline program is in EX0505.C on the supplied disk.

```
/* Illustrates use of data files - reads the base and */
/* height of a triangle from the file bhinp.dat and   */
/* writes the annotated input and calculated area to  */
/* the file resout.dat                                */
#include <stdio.h>
main ()
{
/* Description  ......
   Prepare files for processing
   Read base and height
   Calculate the area of the triangle
   Write the annotated input and result
   Close files
*/
   float base,
         height,
         area ;
   FILE *bhinp = fopen ("bhinp.dat", "r") ;
   FILE *resout = fopen ("resout.dat", "w") ;

   fscanf (bhinp, "%f%f", &base, &height) ;
   area = base * height / 2 ;
   fprintf (resout, "*** AREA OF A TRIANGLE ***\n") ;
   fprintf (resout, "\n") ;
   fprintf (resout, "Base = %.3f\n", base) ;
   fprintf (resout, "Height = %.3f\n", height) ;
   fprintf (resout, "\n") ;
   fprintf (resout, "Calculated area is %.3f\n", area) ;
   fclose (bhinp) ;
   fclose (resout) ;
}
```

Figure 5.2

```
/* To compute the distance between two points */
#include <stdio.h>
#include <math.h>
main ()
{
/* Description  ......
   Prompt for and read coordinates of first point  [cheat025]
   Prompt for and read coordinates of second point [cheat026]
   Compute distance and output it                  [cheat027]
*/

/* variables to hold the two sets of coordinates        */
/* and the distance                         [cheat028] */


}
```

Figure 5.3

```
/* Converts day, month and year to standard date form */
#include <stdio.h>
main ()
{
/* Description  ......
    Ready files for input and output        [cheat029]
    Read in the day, month and year         [cheat030]
    Put year in abbreviated form            [cheat031]
    Output headings                         [cheat032]
    Output input data on three lines        [cheat033]
    Output the date                         [cheat034]
    Output the end message                  [cheat035]
    Close the files                         [cheat036]
*/

/* Identifiers for the input data, the abbreviated    */
/* year and the files                     [cheat037] */


}
```

Figure 5.4

```
/* Program to compute the number of fences and the waste */
/* for a certain length of garden                         */
#include <stdio.h>
main ()
{
/* Description  ......
    Prepare input and output files           [cheat038]
    Read input data                          [cheat039]
    Compute number of full sized fence pieces + 1  [cheat040]
    Compute waste                            [cheat041]
    Output results                           [cheat042]
    Close files                              [cheat043]
*/

/* Identifiers for length of garden, length of each fence,  */
/* waste, number of fences and file pointers     [cheat044] */

}
```

Figure 5.5

6

Selection

6.1 The **if** and **if-else** statements

C contains a mechanism that allows us to choose between different actions according to the value of a condition. The condition must be an expression that yields either a true or false answer. Such an expression may be a single comparison or a compound comparison, where several single comparisons are linked. Let us consider a simple example.

```
if (amount > 0)
    printf ("Valid amount is %d\n", amount) ;
amount += 1 ;
```

would write the contents of the variable amount if its value is positive and then go on to the next statement (add 1 to amount). If the value in amount was zero or negative, then the printf statement would be ignored and the next statement (add 1 to amount) would be processed immediately.

The sequence of operations is:

1. The condition is tested to yield either true or false.
2. The associated statement is executed if and only if the condition is true.
3. Continue with the next statement.

Notice that the statement is introduced by the keyword if, then a condition (or relational expression) in parentheses followed by the statement to be executed when the condition is true. Notice also the layout used in the above example. Though not required by the language, we have indented the statement associated with the if (the printf) to distinguish it from the next statement in the program (amount += 1).

A more extensive form of the selection construct allows us to define an alternative statement that will be executed if the condition is found to be false. For example,

```
if (amount > 0)
    printf ("Valid amount is %d\n", amount) ;
else
    printf ("Amount %d is not valid\n", amount) ;
amount += 1 ;
```

would write the appropriate comment depending on whether the value of amount is greater than zero or not. The statement that adds 1 to amount is always executed.

In this case the sequence of operations is:

1. The condition is tested to yield either true or false.
2. If the condition is true, obey the first printf statement and skip the second statement.
3. If the condition is false, skip the first printf statement, but obey the second statement.
4. Continue with the next statement.

Please note that there is a semicolon following both statements. Also, as a matter of style, both statements have been indented.

6.2   Relational operators

A condition is evaluated (or a comparison made) by comparing the value of an expression with the value of another expression in a number of ways. The type of comparison depends on the relational operator that is used. For instance, we can test for equality or inequality. A full list of the relational operators that one can use in C is now given:

Operator	Meaning
==	is equal to
!=	is not equal to
<	is less than
<=	is less than or equal to
>	is greater than
>=	is greater than or equal to

Notice that four of the above have two characters. These are always written as consecutive characters; there must not be any spaces between them.

Relational operators have the lowest priority of all operators in C, so that the expression

```
(2 * number1 == number2 + number3)
```

is valid. Since == has lower priority than the arithmetic operators it is equivalent to

```
((2 * number1) == (number2 + number3))
```

The relational expression is always enclosed within parentheses. The use of the inner parentheses in the above example, although not necessary, is recommended to make the expression more readable.

In producing relational expressions, we note that a comparison always produces a value of true or false. When we write an expression such as

```
(temperature > boiling)
```

we are making a comparison not stating a fact.

Let us now consider two more selection statements in more detail:

```
if (variable_two > variable_one)
    variable_one = variable_two ;                                       (6-1)
```

This statement will set `variable_one` to the larger of `variable_two` and itself. The condition is tested; either `variable_two` will be greater than `variable_one` or it will not. The condition will either be true or false. If it is true, the value in `variable_two` will be copied into `variable_one`; `variable_one` will now hold the larger value. If the condition is false, the assignment statement is skipped; `variable_one` already held the larger value.

```
if (variable_one > variable_two)
    large = variable_one ;
else
    large = variable_two ;                                              (6-2)
```

Here, the variable `large` is set to the larger of the two values in `variable_one` and `variable_two`. The condition is tested; it will be either true or false. If it is true, `large` is given the value in `variable_one`. If it is false, `large` is given the value in `variable_two`.

Let us now put this into the context of a complete program. Consider the example program in Fig. 6.1. Notice that we also use the indentation technique in the outline design to identify the statement associated with the IF and the statement associated with the ELSE.

6.3   Compound expressions

Conditional (or relational) expressions involving more than a single comparison can be constructed using logical operators. The logical operators available in C are as follows:

```
/* Calculate commission from sales value and commission rate */
#include <stdio.h>
main ()
{
/* Description  ......
   Open input file
   Read sales value and commission rate
   Calculate commission
   Display input values
   IF commission is low
      Display low commission output
   ELSE
      Display high commission output
   Close input file
*/
   float sales_value,
         commission_rate,
         commission ;
   FILE *sales = fopen ("sales.dat", "r") ;

   fscanf (sales, "%f%f", &sales_value, &commission_rate) ;
   commission = sales_value * commission_rate / 100 ;
   printf ("Sales value is %.2f rate is %.2f", sales_value,
      commission_rate) ;
   if (commission <= 10)
      printf (" commission of %.2f is low\n", commission) ;
   else
      printf (" commission of %.2f is high\n", commission) ;
   fclose (sales) ;
}
```

Figure 6.1

Operator	*Meaning*
!	not (that is, negation)
&&	and
||	or

Consider the following examples.

```
if (! (amount == 0))
   printf ("Amount is not zero\n") ;                          (6-3)
```

The effect of ! is to negate the condition following it, that is, it changes false to true or true to false. In this case, the printf statement will only be executed if (! (amount == 0)) is true, which means that (amount == 0) would have to be false. Another way of interpreting this is to say that the printf statement will only be executed if amount equals zero is not true. We could have written the equivalent code as

```
if (amount != 0)
   printf ("Amount is not zero\n") ;
```

which we would interpret as 'if amount not equals zero is true'. The result is the same.

```
if ((amount > 0) && (discount == 25))
   printf ("I will buy it\n") ;                              (6-4)
```

In this statement, we have two conditional expressions joined by the logical operator && (and); this means that both of the simple expressions must be true for the whole compound expression to be true. The printf statement will only be executed if the amount is greater than zero and the discount is exactly equal to 25. If either of these two expressions is false then the printf statement will be skipped.

Note that we have chosen to put both of the simple relational expressions in their own set of parentheses; this is not a requirement of the language, but it helps to make the whole statement more clear. However, recall that the outer parentheses are a necessary part of the language.

```
if ((amount > 0) || (discount == 25))
   printf ("I will think about it\n") ;                      (6-5)
```

Now we have two simple expressions joined by the logical operator || (or). In this case, only one of the simple expressions needs to be true for the result to be true. Therefore, if the amount is greater than zero the printf statement will be executed irrespective of the value of discount. Similarly, if the discount is 25, the printf statement will be executed irrespective of whether the amount is greater than zero or not.

The effect of using these operators is summarized in the table given in Fig. 6.2, where P and Q each represent a conditional expression that could be true or false.

P	Q	!P	P&&Q	P‖Q
true	true	false	true	true
true	false	false	false	true
false	true	true	false	true
false	false	true	false	false

Figure 6.2

We have already seen that there are rules for the order in which arithmetic operators are evaluated. In the case of logical operators, ! (not) has the highest priority, then && (and), then || (or). Let us consider some examples to illustrate these rules.

```
if (! (amount > 0) || (discount == 25))
    printf ("Amount not positive or discount O.K.\n") ;
```
                                                                    (6-6)

will be interpreted as

```
if ((! (amount > 0)) || (discount == 25))
    printf ("Amount not positive or discount O.K.\n") ;
```

If we want to negate the whole of the compound expression, we would need to include parentheses to override the precedence of the ! operator:

```
if (! ((amount > 0) || (discount == 25)))
    printf ("Negative amount and discount O.K.\n") ;
```

```
if ((amount > 0) && (discount == 25) ||
    (discount == 21))
    printf ("Seems like a bargain\n") ;
```
                                                                    (6-7)

The logical operator && has a higher priority than ||, so this condition would be interpreted as

```
if (((amount > 0) && (discount == 25)) ||
    (discount == 21))
    printf ("Seems like a bargain\n") ;
```

It would be evaluated by considering the two simple expressions connected by the && operator first. Thus, the first two expressions amount > 0 and discount == 25 are resolved. If both are true then the printf statement is executed. If either is false then the next expression discount == 21 is evaluated, and if this is true then the printf statement will be obeyed. But is this the effect we want? What should we write if we wanted to display the message when the amount is greater than zero and the discount is either 25 or 21? The solution is shown in Example (6-8) below.

```
if ((amount > 0) && ((discount == 25) ||
    (discount == 21)))
    printf ("Seems like a bargain\n") ;
```
                                                                    (6-8)

Now we have overridden the order of precedence by enclosing the second and third expressions in parentheses. This combined expression will be evaluated first; it will be considered true if the discount is 25 or 21. If it is true and the first expression is true then the message will be displayed.

Many new programmers have some difficulty with compound expressions, especially when inequality is used. Consider part of a program that is required to display the message O.K. when a variable field_a is not equal to 1 or 2:

```
if ((field_a != 1) || (field_a != 2))
    printf ("O.K.\n") ;
```

This does not give the correct meaning. If the value of `field_a` is 2 say, then the first simple expression is true. As the two expressions are connected by `||` (or), the whole compound expression will also be true and the message would be printed, which is not what we require. Similarly, we can also show that the message would be printed when `field_a` is 1.

To give the correct meaning we should write either of the following:

```
if ((field_a != 1) && (field_a != 2))
    printf ("O.K.\n") ;
```

or

```
if (! ((field_a == 1) || (field_a == 2)))
    printf ("O.K.\n") ;
```

It would be constructive to convince yourself that the above two `if` statements are equivalent and correct by using values of 1, 2 and 3 in turn for `field_a`.

We can see from the above that there are alternative ways of coding such examples. Another example is:

```
if (! ((field_a == 5) && (field_b == 6)))
    printf ("O.K.\n") ;
```

which is equivalent to

```
if ((field_a != 5) || (field_b != 6))
    printf ("O.K.\n") ;
```

These examples illustrate the use of two rules called de Morgan's laws, which are now stated formally.

If `C1` and `C2` are conditions:

1. NOT (`C1` OR `C2`) is equivalent to NOT `C1` AND NOT `C2`.
2. NOT (`C1` AND `C2`) is equivalent to NOT `C1` OR NOT `C2`.

A hint for those who find this aspect difficult is to construct the positive condition (which many find conceptually easier), then enclose it in parentheses and precede it by `!` (the negation operator). For example, we may wish to test a code, and if the code is not one of the values 20, 35, 45, we would display a message.

```
((code == 20) || (code == 35) || (code == 45))
```

is the positive condition. Now we negate it:

```
if (! ((code == 20) || (code == 35) || (code == 45)))
    printf ("Code is valid\n") ;
```

6.4   Nested selections

The statements that follow the `if` or the `else` may themselves be conditional
(`if`) statements. This means that we can write programs with many related selections. Consider the following example that writes a suitable message according to
the value of the variable `mark`:

```
if (mark > 70)
    printf ("Distinction") ;
if ((mark <= 70) && (mark >= 40))
    printf ("Pass") ;
if (mark < 40)
    printf ("Fail") ;
```

This would give the correct result, but there is redundancy in the conditions. It is
an example of the common situation where we wish to test for one of several
mutually exclusive conditions. Generally, in this situation, we can write the appropriate code more concisely using `else`, as follows:

```
if (mark > 70)
    printf ("Distinction") ;
else
    if (mark >= 40)
       printf ("Pass") ;
    else
       printf ("Fail") ;
```

Now we are using `if` ... `else` as the second statement of the first `if`
statement. Notice that if the statement of the first `else` is executed it must be that
(`mark` > 70) is false; that is, the mark must be less than or equal to 70.
Consequently, we can simplify the condition for the first alternative to (`mark` >=
40). Similarly, if the statement after the second `else` is executed it must be that
(`mark` >= 40) is false, so the mark must be less than 40. Because of this, we
do not need a condition for the final alternative.

The layout of these so-called *nested* selections is a matter of choice. Many programmers prefer to use a style that puts an `else` followed by an `if` on the same
line. The above example would then be written as follows:

```
if (mark > 70)
   printf ("Distinction") ;
else if (mark >= 40)
   printf ("Pass") ;
else
   printf ("Fail") ;
```

The corresponding outline design for this problem would be

```
IF mark is a distinction
   Display distinction message
ELSE IF mark is a pass
   Display pass message
ELSE (mark is a fail)
   Display fail message
```

Now compare the following pieces of code:

```
if ((amount > 0 ) && (amount > minimum))
   amount -= 1 ;
```
(6-9)

```
if (amount > 0)
   if (amount > minimum)
      amount -= 1 ;
```
(6-10)

Both would appear to have the same effect, that is, decrease amount by 1 provided that it is greater than 0 and greater than minimum. But there is a difference. In Example (6-9), both tests are done at the same level; in Example (6-10), one test is subordinate to the other. The first is more concise and should normally be used. However, sometimes we have to use the second format. For example, consider the following:

```
if ((tally > 0) && (total / tally > target))
   printf ("Acceptable average\n") ;
```

This should be written as:

```
if (tally > 0)
   if (total / tally > target)
      printf ("Acceptable average\n") ;
```

The latter format is necessary in this case because the whole of the compound relational expression in the former is evaluated and this might mean that an illegal division by zero would be executed. (Dividing by zero is impossible to do and so causes the computer to report an error when it is attempted.) In the latter example, no such error could occur; the test that divides tally by total will only be evaluated if tally is greater than zero.

6.5   Compound statements

We have so far assumed that the alternative actions are single statements. If we want the action of an if statement or either action of an if...else statement (that is, true or false paths) to consist of a number of statements, then we use braces {...} to make a sequence of statements into a single compound statement.

The program given as Fig. 6.3 compares a request for funds with the amount remaining in an account and decides whether to allow the request. Note where we do and do not have semicolons; in particular, there is no semicolon after either }

```
/* Program to examine bank balance */
#include <stdio.h>
main ()
{
/* Description  ......
   Obtain account balance
   Obtain withdrawal amount
   IF sufficient funds for withdrawal
      Display authorization message
      Update account balance
      Display updated account balance
   ELSE
      Display refusal message
      Display account balance
*/
   int account_balance,
       withdrawal ;

   printf ("Enter account balance: ") ;
   scanf ("%d", &account_balance) ;
   printf ("Enter withdrawal amount: ") ;
   scanf ("%d", &withdrawal) ;
   if (account_balance >= withdrawal)
      {
      printf ("Transaction authorised\n") ;
      account_balance -= withdrawal ;
      printf ("New balance is : %d\n", account_balance) ;
      }
   else
      {
      printf ("No chance!!\n") ;
      printf ("Only %d left\n", account_balance) ;
      }
}
```

Figure 6.3

(right brace). Also, notice that for compound statements we have used the indentation convention that we introduced earlier for single statements.

We do not use braces in the outline design; here we rely on the indentation to
convey the appropriate meaning.

Braces can also be used with a single statement, which is sometimes useful in
nested if statements to make the code more readable. Consider the following
statement:

```
if (amount > 25)
if (discount < 5) price = 7 ;
else price = 9 ;
```

To which `if` does the `else` belong? The `else` goes with the nearest available `if`. Of course, using correct indentation would have helped.

```
if (amount > 25)
   if (discount < 5)
      price = 7 ;
   else
      price = 9 ;
```

If we wanted to override the rule concerning `else`, we could use braces as follows:

```
if (amount > 25)
   {
   if (discount < 5)
      price = 7 ;
   }
else
   price = 9 ;
```

Convince yourself that we have now produced two entirely different selection conditions by applying data to both. Note that for both solutions there are three possible outcomes in respect to `price`. It may be given a value of 7, or a value of 9, or its value may not be changed.

Exercises

1. Refer to the program in Fig. 6.1, then answer the following questions.
   (i) Why is the space character immediately before the word commission in the `printf` statements necessary?
   (ii) How many times would you need to run the program to test it?
   (iii) Why is it advisable to avoid using tests for equality when testing real numbers?
2. Evaluate the following relational expressions by indicating whether they are true or false. Assume that variables have been assigned as follows:

```
code = 4 ;
amount = 0 ;
figure = -1 ;
```

   (i)   `(code != 3)`
   (ii) `((code != 3) && (amount == 0))`
   (iii) `((figure >= 0) || (amount >= 0))`
   (iv) `(((code == 4) || (figure == 2)) && (amount >= 0))`
   (v)   `(! ((amount > 0) || (code >= 4)))`
   (vi) `(! ((amount > 0) && (code >= 4)))`

3. Complete the program given as Fig. 6.4. The program is to read two integers from a data file and display a suitable message if the first integer has a value greater than 50. Also, if the value of the first integer is less than the second then an appropriate message is displayed. When you have completed the coding task, use the editor to insert your lines of code into your copy of the file EX0603.C. When this is done, you should attempt to compile and run the program. Run it a few times with different data.

4. An examination mark and the pass mark are read from the keyboard. Fig. 6.5 gives an outline design for a program that displays a message of congratulation or commiseration depending on whether the mark is a pass or a fail. As usual, when you have completed the program, you should use the computer to check your coded solution. The outline design for the solution is found in EX0604.C on the enclosed disk. You need to devise your own test data, which should consist of a minimum of three different cases.

5. Using the outline design to be found in Fig. 6.6, produce the program coding to input two integer values (A and B) from the keyboard and produce output according to these values as follows. If either value is zero, display the message ERROR: Zero values; otherwise output A, B and their product. Also, provided that neither value is zero, calculate A − B and A + B, and output an appropriate message depending on whether the difference is greater than or less than the sum. EX0605.C contains the outline design for you to edit in the usual way.

6. The outline design in Fig. 6.7 relates to the problem of establishing the pools value for a given football match result. The home goals and away goals are read from the keyboard (as integers) and validated (that is, tested to be in the range 0 to 20 inclusive). If invalid, an appropriate error message is displayed, otherwise the pools value and match result are displayed in an appropriate way (you may choose your own teams). The pools value is 1.5 for a home win, 1.5 for an away win, 2.0 for a no-score draw, 3.0 for a draw of one goal each, and 2.5 for any other drawn result.

   After carefully coding and checking, produce appropriate test data cases, then use EX0606.C as the basis for implementing your solution.

```
/* Read two integers and display suitable messages */
#include <stdio.h>
main ()
{
/* Description  ......
   Prepare input file and read first integer    [cheat045]
   IF first integer greater than 50             [cheat046]
      Display integer over 50 message
   Read second integer                          [cheat047]
   IF first integer less than second integer    [cheat048]
      Display first < second message
   Close input file                             [cheat049]
*/

/* variables for integers                       [cheat050] */


}
```

Figure 6.4

```
/* Tests an exam. mark and displays pass or fail message */
#include <stdio.h>
main ()
{
/* Description  ......
   Prompt for and read exam mark and pass mark   [cheat052]
   IF exam mark is a pass                        [cheat053]
      Display congratulatory message
   ELSE (exam mark is a fail )                   [cheat054]
      Display message of commiseration
*/

/* Variables for exam mark and pass mark         [cheat055] */


}
```

Figure 6.5

```
/* To demonstrate if...else and compound statements */
#include <stdio.h>
main ()
{
/* Description  ......
   Prompt for and input two values into A,B     [cheat056]
   IF either A or B is zero                      [cheat057]
      Display error message
   ELSE (A and B valid)                          [cheat058]
      Display A,B and A*B                        [cheat059]
      Compute sum and difference of A,B          [cheat060]
      IF sum (A,B) > difference (A,B)            [cheat061]
         Display sum > difference message
      ELSE (sum < difference)                    [cheat062]
         Display sum < difference message
*/

/* Variables as appropriate                      [cheat063] */



}
```

Figure 6.6

```
/* To display match result and pools value given home */
/* and away goals                                    */
#include <stdio.h>
main ()
{
/* Description  ......
   Prompt for and read home and away goals     [cheat064]
   IF goals are valid values (0-20)            [cheat065]
      IF not a draw                            [cheat066]
         pools value is 1.5
      ELSE IF no score draw
         pools value is 2.0
      ELSE IF one all draw
         pools value is 3.0
      ELSE (other draw result)
         pools value is 2.5
      Display match result and pools value     [cheat067]
   ELSE (invalid goals values)                 [cheat068]
      Display error message
*/

/* Variables for home & away goals, pools value [cheat069] */



}
```

Figure 6.7

7

Repetition

7.1 The `while` statement

We have seen that programming requires the ability to make decisions. Another facility often needed is the ability to repeat actions. In fact, programs that process several similar items are more common than those that just process one data item.

The term *iteration* is often used to mean a series of repetitions of one or more actions. All programs must eventually finish, hence there must be some method for terminating an iteration. For example, a sequence of positive data items could be terminated by a negative value (the end marker). We could then say that processing should continue so long as (that is, while) the value read in is positive.

The fundamental repetitive control structure in C is the `while` statement. Consider the following example, which assumes that the input file contains some integers with zero as an end marker.

```
fscanf (infile, "%d", &amount) ;
while (amount != 0)
    {
    printf ("%d\n", amount) ;
    fscanf (infile, "%d", &amount) ;
    }
printf ("End marker reached\n") ;
```

An amount is read; if the amount is not zero the repetition starts, otherwise the comment End marker reached is displayed. The two statements that display the amount and read another amount are executed repeatedly while the amount is not zero. When an amount of zero is reached, the repetition stops and the next statement is obeyed.

Note that the condition (relational expression) must be enclosed within parentheses, and must give a true result for the associated statement to be obeyed. The

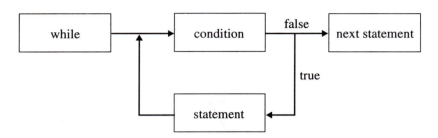

Figure 7.1

sequence of operations is:

1. The condition is tested to yield either true or false.
2. If the result is false, the statements in braces are skipped and the program continues at the next statement.
3. If the result is true, the statements in braces are executed, then the above is repeated from (1).

This can be represented by the diagram given as Fig. 7.1. The statement associated with the `while` is most often a compound statement, that is, a sequence of statements enclosed by braces; but it is not necessarily so.

The condition must eventually give a false result (that is, not true), otherwise we would have a situation in which the loop continues an infinite number of times. The statement to be repeated should eventually do something to make the condition false; for example, as in the above, where a value of zero for `amount` must eventually be read.

If the condition is false when it is first tested, the loop will not be executed.

An important general technique for processing an arbitrary length list of data values can be expressed in the form of an outline design as follows:

```
Initialization (e.g. set total(s) to zero)
Read the first value (or, get first item)
WHILE continuing condition (not terminating condition)
    Process the current value or item
    Read the next value (or, get the next item)
Finalization (e.g. produce end-results)
```

Note that the indentation indicates the processing that is contained within the `while` loop.

The example given as Fig. 7.2 illustrates this technique. Notice how the outline design in Fig. 7.2 follows the general pattern. Also, observe the read-ahead technique. We must read a value before we can test whether or not we have reached the end marker. This means that we read a value immediately before

```
    /* Calculate mean (average) of a list of positive numbers */
    #include <stdio.h>
    main ()
    {
    /* Description  ......
       Open input file
       Initialize running total and count to zero
       Read first number
       WHILE number is positive (not end of list)
           Add number to running total
           Increment count of numbers
           Read next number
       IF count of numbers > 0
           Calculate mean
           Display count and mean
       ELSE
           Display error message
       Close input file
    */
       float current_number,
             running_total = 0,
             mean ;
       int    count = 0 ;
       FILE *numbers = fopen ("numbers.dat", "r") ;

1      fscanf (numbers, "%f", &current_number) ;
2      while (current_number > 0)
           {
3          running_total += current_number ;
4          count += 1 ;
5          fscanf (numbers, "%f", &current_number) ;
           }
6      if (count > 0)
           {
7          mean = running_total / count ;
8          printf ("%d numbers read. Mean = %.2f\n", count, mean) ;
           }
       else
9          printf ("No numbers read\n") ;
       fclose (numbers) ;
    }
```

Figure 7.2

entering the loop and we must read the next value as soon as the current value has been processed within the loop. In this particular example, Process current item consists of just two actions; in other problems it could represent a far more lengthy process.

This program is correct even when the input file contains only the end marker.

Statement number	Variables				Conditions	
	current_number	running_total	mean	count	current_number >0	count >0
declaration		0.0		0		
1	4.7					
2					true	
3		4.7				
4				1		
5	2.1					
2					true	
3		6.8				
4				2		
5	5.5					
2					true	
3		12.3				
4				3		
5	−1					
2					false	
6						true
7			4.1			
8						

Figure 7.3

Statement number	Variables				Conditions	
	current_number	running_total	mean	count	current_number >0	count >0
declaration		0.0		0		
1	−1					
2					false	
6						false
9						

Figure 7.4

In this case, the first value read is negative, hence the condition for the while loop, (current_number > 0), is false, so the body of the loop is never executed.

To convince yourself of the correctness of the example in Fig. 7.2, work through the trace tables given as Figs 7.3 and 7.4. The trace table in Fig. 7.3 assumes that the input file contains the values 4.7, 2.1, 5.5, −1. The trace table in

```
/* Outputs first 10 integers and their squares as a table */
#include <stdio.h>
main ()
{
/* Description  ......
   Display headings
   Define (get) first number
   WHILE not at the end of the numbers
        Compute N squared and display it
        Define (get) next number
*/
   const int last_value = 10 ;

   int       current_number,
             current_number_squared ;

   printf (" N     N squared\n\n") ;
   current_number = 1 ;
   while (current_number <= last_value)
       {
       current_number_squared = current_number * current_number ;
       printf ("%3d %10d\n", current_number,
           current_number_squared) ;
       current_number += 1 ;
       }
}
```

Figure 7.5

Fig. 7.4 assumes the single value −1 in the input file.

The example given in Fig. 7.5 is a program that prints the first ten positive integers together with their squares below appropriate headings. Now we are dealing with a known number of values. Nevertheless, the structure of the program follows the same pattern as the general outline given above and the example in Fig. 7.2. In this case, we replace the reads with:

```
Define (get) first number (current_number = 1)
Define (get) next number  (current_number += 1)
```

In this example we notice that not only are we dealing with a known number of values, but that the loop is controlled by a counting mechanism. This is such a common feature in programming that a special count-controlled loop construct is often provided by programming languages. C is no exception, as we shall see in Chapter 9.

7.2   Nested control structures

A programming problem will often require both repetition and selection, possibly with selection enclosed (or nested) within repetition or vice versa. The nesting

```
/* Find the largest number from a list */
#include <stdio.h>
main ()
{
/* Description  ......
   Open input file
   Read first value, make it the largest
   WHILE not at the end of the list
       IF current value > largest so far
          make current value to be the largest
       Read next value
   Display largest number
   Close input file
*/
   int  current_value,
        largest ;
   FILE *list = fopen ("list.dat", "r") ;

   fscanf (list, "%d", &current_value) ;
   largest = current_value ;
   while (current_value != 9999)
      {
      if (current_value > largest)
         largest = current_value ;
      fscanf (list, "%d", &current_value) ;
      }
   printf ("Largest number is %d \n", largest) ;
   fclose (list) ;
}
```

Figure 7.6

may involve several levels. Since the `while` and `if` constructs both contain statements and are themselves statements, we can build up the required nesting.

The program shown in Fig. 7.6 indicates how an `if` statement can be nested within a `while` statement. The program finds the largest value from an arbitrary length list of integers. The integer 9999 is used as an end marker.

The next example, shown as Fig. 7.7, uses a `while` statement nested within another `while` statement. The program computes and prints, as a whole number, the average of the number of customers visiting a supermarket's checkouts for each day. The data are held in an input file. In each line there is a set of data for each day. Each set contains integer readings giving the number of customers using each opened checkout, and is terminated by −1. The file is terminated by a single line containing −9. For example, the file

```
53  62  12  −1
−1
61  75  33  41  −1
−9
```

would give

```
Day 1 42
Day 2 no readings
Day 3 52
```

Notice the same general pattern outlined in the previous section emerges in the outline description and hence in the C source code for both the inner and outer loop. The outer loop processes all of the data for a day repetitively until the end-of-file marker is reached. The inner loop processes an individual reading repetitively until the end-of-day marker is reached.

Exercises

1. Refer to the program in Fig. 7.2, then answer the following questions.
   (i) What change would you make to the relational expression in the `while` statement if the end marker was changed to 9999?
   (ii) Why is the `if` statement necessary?
   (iii) What would happen if the second `fscanf` statement was missing?
   (iv) What would happen if the first `fscanf` statement was missing?
2. Refer to the program in Fig. 7.5, then answer the following questions.
   (i) What change(s) would be necessary to display the first 20 integers and their squares?
   (ii) What changes would be necessary to display the first 10 even numbers and their squares?
   (iii) What is the effect of `\n\n` in the first `printf` statement?
3. Refer to the program in Fig. 7.6, then answer the following questions.
   (i) What would be the effect of changing the relational expression of the `while` statement to `(! (current_value == 9999))`?
   (ii) What changes should be made so that the program finds the smallest number from a list?
   (iii) How else might the variable `largest` be initialized?
4. Refer to the program in Fig. 7.7, then answer the following questions.
   (i) Why is the first `fscanf` statement outside the main loop?
   (ii) What are the purposes of the initialization statements for the inner loop?
5. Use the outline design given in Fig. 7.8 and EX0705.C on the supplied disk to complete the interactive program that reads in a positive integer, n say, and from this produces the n-times table up to times 12. The input should be validated to be in the range 2 to 12. The output should be of the form:

```
n-Times Table
   1 x n = p
   2 x n = q
   .  .  .  .  .
  12 x n = z
```

6. Figure 7.9 (and EX0706.C on the supplied disk) contains an outline design for a program that reads the file EX0706.DAT. The file contains a list of values representing units of electricity consumed for different customers. The list is concluded by an end marker of a negative number. The program produces, on the screen, a table below headings showing the units consumed and corresponding charge. The charging policy is to charge 5p per unit for the first 60 units consumed and 2p per unit for the remainder for each customer. Complete the program and test it with the specified test data file.

7. Figure 7.10 (and EX0707.C) contains the design for a program that reads the file EX0707.DAT, containing a list of integer numbers terminated by 9999, and displays on the screen those numbers that are repeated consecutively. For example, from the list 3 5 5 7 8 4 2 2 5 6 6 9 4 2, the output would be 5 2 6. Complete this program and test it with the specified file.

8. The sales figures for a number of salesmen are recorded in the file EX0708.DAT as follows:

```
35 532 -1
762 630 542 601 -1
241 61 320 -1
35 -1
43 48 49 50 53 55 -1
-9
```

where each line represents the data for each salesman and the figures on each line are sales figures achieved for a variable number of months. The −1 indicates the end of a salesman's details. The −9 indicates the end of file.

Figure 7.11 (and EX0708.C) contains the outline design for a program to compute and display with appropriate text the total sales for each salesman (identifying them by Salesman 1, Salesman 2 etc.) and also a grand total of all sales in the file.

```
/* Computes average number of customers at checkouts */
#include <stdio.h>
main ()
{
/* Description  ......
   Open files
   Initialise day number = 0
   Read first reading
   WHILE sets to process (reading not = -9)
      Initialize number of readings per set
      Initialize total readings for set = zero
      WHILE readings to process (reading not = -1)
         Accumulate total readings for set
         Increment no. of readings per set
         Read next reading
      Increment day number
      Write day number
      IF no readings in current set
         Write 'no readings'
      ELSE
         Write truncated average of readings
      Read next reading
   Close files
*/
      int   day_number,
            number_of_readings,
            total_readings,
            current_reading ;
      FILE *checkout = fopen ("checkout.dat", "r") ;
      FILE *results = fopen ("results.dat", "w") ;

      day_number = 0 ;
      fscanf (checkout, "%d", &current_reading) ;
      while (current_reading != -9)
         {
         number_of_readings = 0 ;
         total_readings = 0 ;
         while (current_reading != -1)
            {
            total_readings += current_reading ;
            number_of_readings += 1 ;
            fscanf (checkout, "%d", &current_reading) ;
            }
         day_number += 1 ;
         fprintf (results, "Day %d", day_number) ;
         if (number_of_readings == 0)
            fprintf (results, " no readings\n") ;
         else
            fprintf (results, " %d \n", total_readings /
               number_of_readings) ;
         fscanf (checkout, "%d", &current_reading) ;
         }
      fclose (checkout) ;
      fclose (results) ;
}
```

Figure 7.7

```
/* To produce any specified times table upto 12 */
#include <stdio.h>
main ()
{
/* Description ......
    Prompt for and read table number          [cheat070]
    IF table number valid                      [cheat071]
        Display table heading                  [cheat072]
        Define first multiplier                [cheat073]
        WHILE not at the end of the table      [cheat074]
            Calculate and display table line   [cheat075]
            Define next multiplier             [cheat076]
    ELSE                                        [cheat077]
        Display error message
*/

/* Variables as required                       [cheat078] */


}
```

Figure 7.8

```
/* To produce a list of units consumed and associated charges */
#include <stdio.h>
main ()
{
/* Description ......
    Prepare input file and read first units consumed  [cheat079]
    Display column headings                           [cheat080]
    WHILE not at the end marker                        [cheat081]
        IF number of units greater than 60            [cheat082]
            Calculate charge when units at both rates [cheat083]
        ELSE                                          [cheat084]
            Calculate charge, units at high rate only
        Display units and charge                      [cheat085]
        Read next units consumed                      [cheat086]
    Close input file                                  [cheat087]
*/

/* High and low rates as constants                    [cheat088] */

/* Variables as required                              [cheat089] */


}
```

Figure 7.9

```
/* Select numbers repeated consecutively in a list */
#include <stdio.h>
main ()
{
/* Description ......
    Prepare input file and read first number      [cheat090]
    Display headings                              [cheat091]
    Initialize previous number (to 9999)          [cheat092]
    WHILE not at the end of the file              [cheat093]
        IF current number = previous number       [cheat094]
            Display current number
        Set previous number from current number    [cheat095]
        Read next number                          [cheat096]
    Close input file                              [cheat097]
*/

/* End marker constant                           [cheat098] */

/* Variables as required                         [cheat099] */


}
```

Figure 7.10

```
/* Computes salesmen's total sales and grand total */
#include <stdio.h>
main ()
{
/* Description ......
    Open sales file                                     [cheat100]
    Read first sales figure                             [cheat101]
    Initialize sales grand total = 0                    [cheat102]
    Initialize salesman number = 0                      [cheat103]
    WHILE salesmen to process (sales not = -9)          [cheat104]
        Initialize salesman's total = 0                 [cheat105]
        WHILE sales figures to process (sales not = -1) [cheat106]
            Accumulate sales figure                     [cheat107]
            Read next sales figure                      [cheat108]
        Increase salesman number by 1                   [cheat109]
        Display a salesman's total                      [cheat110]
        Read next sales figure                          [cheat111]
    Display grand total                                 [cheat112]
    Close sales file                                    [cheat113]
*/

/* Variables as appropriate                       [cheat114] */

}
```

Figure 7.11

8

Characters and strings

8.1 The data type `char`

So far we have dealt mainly with numeric values; however, a great deal of programming involves processing character data. For example, an editor program manipulates characters in files. To write programs that manipulate characters we need constants and variables whose values are *characters*.

A value of type `char` is a single element of a finite and ordered set of characters. This is illustrated by Fig. 8.1, which contains part of the set used by most computers in the form of a table. The column and row headings are explained later.

A constant of type `char` is denoted by a single character enclosed in apostrophes, for example

```
'A'  '*'  '2'  ' '
```

We can declare character constants and variables as follows:

```
const char blank = ' ',
           query = '?' ;
const char zed = 'Z' ;
```

	0	1	2	3	4	5	6	7	8	9	10	11	12	13	14	15
32		!	"	£	$	%	&	'	(	)	*	+	,	–	.	/
48	0	1	2	3	4	5	6	7	8	9	:	;	<	=	>	?
64	@	A	B	C	D	E	F	G	H	I	J	K	L	M	N	O
80	P	Q	R	S	T	U	V	W	X	Y	Z	[	\	]	^	_
96	blank	a	b	c	d	e	f	g	h	i	j	k	l	m	n	o
112	p	q	r	s	t	u	v	w	x	y	z	{			}	~	

Figure 8.1

```
char ch1,
     character ;
char initial ;
```

We can assign character values to variables, for example

```
character = blank ;
initial = 'A' ;
ch1 = '8' ;
character = initial ;
```

It is important to appreciate the difference between the following two statements:

```
thisvalue = 'A' ;                                              (8-1)
thisvalue = A ;                                                (8-2)
```

In (8-1) we have an assignment of the character value A to the character variable
thisvalue. In (8-2) we have the assignment of the contents of the variable A to
the variable thisvalue.

Similarly, you should recognize the difference between the following statements:

```
thisvalue = '7' ;                                              (8-3)
thisvalue = 7 ;                                                (8-4)
```

In (8-3) we have an assignment of the character value 7 to the character variable
thisvalue. In (8-4) the integer value 7 is assigned to the numeric variable
thisvalue.

Character values can be transmitted by means of the standard functions scanf,
fscanf, printf and fprintf. For example, assuming that char_value is
a variable of type char, we might write the following:

```
scanf ("%c", &char_value) ;
```

This will take a single character from the keyboard, and store it in char_value.
Notice the control string format specification of %c to denote a character.

We have seen that in the reading of numeric values (int or float) from either
the keyboard or a file, any so-called white space characters (that is, blank or
newline or tab) are skipped over. However, the white space characters are specific
values of the data type char. Thus white space characters are not skipped by
scanf or fscanf when reading characters; the next character from the input
data, whether a white space character or not, is the one that will be stored in
char_value.

Consider the following simple program fragment:

```
fscanf (inp_file, "%c", &char_value) ;
while (char_value != 'Z')
```

```
{
printf ("Character is %c\n", char_value) ;
fscanf (inp_file, "%c", &char_value) ;
}
```

If the input file contained

```
ABZ
```

followed by a newline, the output would be

```
Character is A
Character is B
```

However, if the same input file contained

```
A
B
Z
```

with each letter followed by a newline, the output would be

```
Character is A
Character is
```
                        (a blank line)
```
Character is B
Character is
```
                        (a blank line)

This illustrates that the newline character is read just like any other character and in the above example is output within the loop. If we wish to ignore newline characters in such situations, we can use the following technique:

```
fscanf (inp_file, "%c", &char_value) ;
while (char_value != 'Z')
    {
    printf ("Character is %c\n", char_value) ;
    fscanf (inp_file, "\n%c", &char_value) ;
    }
```

Now, by inserting the \n in the format string of the second fscanf, the newline character from the previous line is skipped over before the next character is read.

The function fprintf will output characters to a file and printf is used to display characters on the monitor screen. For example,

```
printf ("%c", char_value) ;
```

will display the character stored in char_value. Again, %c in the control string denotes a character. Only the single character contained in char_value is displayed; apostrophes are not displayed before and after the value. The convention of enclosing character values in apostrophes is used only within the text of a C program. As we have seen, this is necessary to distinguish a character value from a C identifier name with just one letter, and to distinguish a character value from a numeric value of just one digit.

We can use a field width when outputting characters. For example,

```
printf ("%12c", char_value) ;
```

will display 11 blanks followed by the character stored in `char_value`.

```
fprintf (outfile, "%14c", ' ') ;
```

would write 14 spaces.

Most computers use the ASCII character codes. ASCII is the acronym given to an international standard concerned with the communication of data. It assigns to each character in a specific set a unique numeric value to identify it. This value can be determined by finding the character in the table in Fig. 8.1 and adding the number in its row and column. For example,

'A' through 'Z' have values 65 to 90
'a' through 'z' have values 97 to 122
'0' through '9' have values 48 to 57

In C, characters can be compared by means of the standard relational operators, shown again here:

```
==   !=   <   <=   >   >=
```

The ordering of the character set is determined by the corresponding numeric value of each character. This means that normal alphabetic ordering is preserved (A comes before B, and B comes before C). Hence the following expressions will give the result that we would expect (that is, will yield true):

```
('A' < 'B')
('B' < 'C')
```

Numerical ordering for digits is preserved:

```
('0' < '1') and
('1' < '2')
```

both yield true. Also, notice that the following would yield true:

```
('A' < 'a')
('Y' < 'c')
('9' < 'w')
```

Let us consider the sample program shown in Fig. 8.2. An input file contains a list of characters on one line terminated by a ; (semicolon) or a . (full stop). The program writes all the input except the end marker to the output file and then the number of upper-case (capital) letters and the number of digits.

```
/* Counts the capital letters and digits in an input file */
#include <stdio.h>
main ()
{
/* Descripton  ......
   Open files
   Read the first character
   WHILE not file terminating characters
       Process a character
       Read next character
   Output results
   Close files
*/
   int   letter_count = 0,
         digit_count = 0 ;
   char  current_character ;
   FILE *inpfile = fopen ("inpfile.dat", "r") ;
   FILE *outpfile = fopen ("outpfile.dat", "w") ;

   fscanf (inpfile, "%c", &current_character) ;
   while (!((current_character == ';') ||
      (current_character == '.')))
      {
      fprintf (outpfile, "%c", current_character) ;
      if ((current_character >= 'A') &&
         (current_character <= 'Z'))
         letter_count += 1 ;
      else if ((current_character >= '0') &&
         (current_character <= '9'))
         digit_count += 1 ;
      fscanf (inpfile, "%c", &current_character) ;
      }
   fprintf (outpfile, "\nThere are %d capital letters",
      letter_count) ;
   fprintf (outpfile, " and %d digits\n", digit_count) ;
   fclose (inpfile) ;
   fclose (outpfile) ;
}
```

Figure 8.2

8.2   Strings

We have already met strings when we considered the output of text. For example,

```
printf ("Please input a number: ") ;
```

illustrates the use of a string constant and demonstrates that it is included between quotes. This string constant is 24 characters long, the 23 characters you see and a null character (represented in C by \0) as an invisible end character. Strings need an end character because they are conceptually of variable length. We can illustrate this better by considering some declarations for string variables.

String variables are declared formally as one-dimensional arrays of type char. Arrays are fully explained in Chapter 13, but at this stage the reader only needs to understand the following examples:

```
char street [24],
     town [24] ;
char symbol_1 [10],
     symbol_2 [8] ;
```

Notice that when declaring a string variable we specify, in brackets, its maximum length including one character for the end marker (\0). However, strings stored in these variables can vary in length; street could hold any string value up to 23 characters in length and symbol_1 any string value up to 9 characters in length.

Strings differ from the data types that we have already come across insofar as we do not use the assignment operator (=). The function strcpy, an abbreviation for string copy, is used to make string assignments:

```
strcpy (symbol_1, "***") ;
strcpy (symbol_2, symbol_1) ;
strcpy (street, "Coronation Street") ;
strcpy (town, "Liverpool") ;
```

The contents of the second string are copied into the first string, completely overwriting it. After the first two statements, therefore, both symbol_1 and symbol_2 would contain three asterisks.

The function strcpy is found in string.h, so we need to write an include statement at the start of our program:

```
#include <string.h>
```

In the printf and fprintf statements we use the %s format specification in the control string. Remember that any spaces included within this control string are output, but the output stops when the null character (\0) is reached for each string. Hence the statement

```
printf ("%s, %s\n", street, town) ;
```

would display

```
Coronation Street, Liverpool
```

We can use fscanf and scanf to read strings from files or the keyboard respectively. Using the string variable declarations above, we could write the following statement:

```
scanf ("%s%s", street, town) ;
```

This would cause data to be read such that all characters up to the next white-space character would be input to `street`, all of the white-space characters would be skipped, and then the next set of characters up to the next white space would be input to `town`. (Recall that the white space character that ends the input strings may be a blank, a tab character or the newline <ENTER> character.) For the above `scanf` statement it would be likely that the keyboard operator would type either on two lines,

```
Merseyview
Liverpool
```

or on one line, as follows:

```
Merseyview Liverpool
```

When the space, tab or newline character is encountered C will place a `\0` character at the end of the string for you. One seemingly strange difference between the above `scanf` statement and those we have met before is the absence of an `&` character before each of the variables. This is deliberate and necessary

```
/* Program to demonstrate reading and comparing strings */
#include <stdio.h>
#include <string.h>
main ()
{
/* Description  ......
   Open input file
   Read first pair of strings
   WHILE not end-of-file marker strings
      Process current strings
      Get next pair of strings
   Close input file
*/
   char first_string [6],
        second_string [6] ;
   FILE *inpfile = fopen ("inpfile.dat", "r") ;

   fscanf (inpfile, "%s%s", first_string, second_string) ;
   while (! ((strcmp (first_string, "ZZZZZ") == 0) &&
         (strcmp (second_string, "ZZZZZ") == 0)))
      {
      printf ("First string is '%s'\n", first_string) ;
      printf ("Second string is '%s'\n", second_string) ;
      fscanf (inpfile, "%s%s", first_string, second_string) ;
      }
   fclose (inpfile) ;
}
```

Figure 8.3

because of the way in which data are placed in string variables. The technical distinctions will be explained later.

Let us now consider the example program given in Fig. 8.3. For this program let us suppose we have an input file containing the following lines:

```
Jimmy  Fred
Bill Willy
Hanah  Me
ZZZZZ ZZZZZ
```

We would get the following results:

```
First string is 'Jimmy'
Second string is 'Fred'
First string is 'Bill'
Second string is 'Willy'
First string is 'Hanah'
Second string is 'Me'
```

Notice we have got truly variable length strings to a maximum of 6 characters including the invisible \0. If the input contained strings greater than 5 characters in length the fscanf would still attempt to input them to the string variable, but this would cause an error. As we shall see later, there are techniques that can be used to ensure that string variables are not 'overfilled'. We will assume for the moment that we only have 'well-behaved' input.

One new function is introduced in this program. Strings cannot be compared using the usual relational operators. We use instead the strcmp (string compare) function. This is found in string.h, so we need to write an include statement at the start of our program (see the third line). Comparison of strings is defined by the normal lexicographic convention based on the ordering of the character set. The strcmp function takes two arguments: the string identifiers and/or string values to be compared. The result is an integer less than zero if the first string is lexically less than the second string (in the same way that in a telephone directory 'Jones' is lexically less than 'Smith' and so comes nearer the beginning of the names list). The result is equal to zero if the strings have the same lexical value (that is, they are identical), or greater than zero if the first string is lexically greater than the second string. This can be summarized as follows:

We must use	*Instead of*
(strcmp (stringa, stringb) < 0)	(stringa < stringb)
(strcmp (stringa, stringb) == 0)	(stringa == stringb)
(strcmp (stringa, stringb) > 0)	(stringa > stringb)

In Fig. 8.3 we have

```
while (! ((strcmp (first_string, "ZZZZZ") == 0) &&
         (strcmp (second_string, "ZZZZZ") == 0)))
```

In this particular example, we want the iteration to terminate when both first_string and second_string are equal to ZZZZZ. So the condition for continuing the iteration is the negation of this. Notice that we have tested for equality of first_string with ZZZZZ by testing for equality of the result from strcmp with zero (and similarly for second_string).

Let us consider another example. A class file contains a number of lines (records), each containing the sex of a student (M or F), followed by the age of the student, followed by a space, followed by the student's name. It is required to print a class list showing the name then the age and sex, with the average ages of both males and females at the end. An example of the class file is

```
M10 Stevens
F12 Wagner
M17 Rancourt
F14 Wagner
F17 Harold
Z00 Z
```

The last line is a dummy line to indicate the end of the file. Note that the space after the age is not strictly necessary because a fscanf statement would recognize the end of the integers that represent age when it came to a non-integer value. If a space is present, it will be skipped when fscanf reads the string value for the student's name.

The results from the above would be

```
Stevens 10 M
Wagner 12 F
Rancourt 17 M
Wagner 14 F
Harold 17 F

Average age of boys : 13.5

Average age of girls : 14.3
```

Fig. 8.4 contains the program to implement a solution to this problem. Let us examine this in some detail. First we note that the declarations include:

```
char    name [12] ;
int     age ;
char    sex ;
```

These variables will hold the contents of each input line. We have declared a string variable to hold the student's name and have defined it as having a maximum of 12 characters, including the end marker for the string. Now let us examine the input and output statements.

```
fscanf (classfile, "%c%d%s", &sex, &age, name) ;
```

```c
/* Lists students and calculates average ages */
#include <stdio.h>
main ()
{
/* Description  ......
   Ready files and read first line
   Initialize counts
   WHILE not end of the class file
      Process a student's details
      Read next line
   Process and output averages
   Close files
*/
   char   name [12] ;
   int    age ;
   char   sex ;                    /* M or F */
   int    boys_total_age,
          girls_total_age,
          number_of_boys,
          number_of_girls ;
   float  average_boys_age,
          average_girls_age ;
   FILE *classfile = fopen ("class.dat", "r") ;
   FILE *list = fopen ("list.dat", "w") ;

   fscanf (classfile, "%c%d%s", &sex, &age, name) ;
   boys_total_age = 0 ;
   girls_total_age = 0 ;
   number_of_boys = 0 ;
   number_of_girls = 0 ;
   while (sex != 'Z')
      {
      fprintf (list, "%s %2d %c\n", name, age, sex) ;
      if (sex == 'M')
         {
         number_of_boys += 1 ;
         boys_total_age += age ;
         }
      else
         {
         number_of_girls += 1 ;
         girls_total_age += age ;
         }
      fscanf (classfile, "\n%c%d%s", &sex, &age, name) ;
      }
   if (number_of_boys > 0)
      average_boys_age = (float) boys_total_age / number_of_boys ;
   else
      average_boys_age = 0.0 ;
   fprintf (list, "\nAverage age of boys : %.1f\n",
      average_boys_age) ;
   if (number_of_girls > 0)
      average_girls_age = (float) girls_total_age / number_of_girls ;
   else
      average_girls_age = 0.0 ;
   fprintf (list, "\nAverage age of girls : %.1f\n",
      average_girls_age) ;
   fclose (list) ;
   fclose (classfile) ;
}
```

Figure 8.4

This is the input statement for reading the first line. The control string specifies three format specifications. The %c indicates that a character is to be input, %d indicates an integer and %s indicates a string is to be input from the input file. Arguments three, four and five specify the variables into which the input data are to be placed. Notice that, for character and integer input, we must place a & before the variable identifier, but for string input we do not.

```
fscanf (classfile, "\n%c%d%s", &sex, &age, name) ;
```

This is the input statement for reading the next line (within the loop). The control string now specifies the same three format specifications, but preceded by \n to indicate that a newline character will need to be skipped from the previous line because the first variable (sex) is of type char.

```
fprintf (list, "%s %2d %c\n", name, age, sex) ;
```

This statement outputs to the file list.dat the name, age and sex. Notice the control string indicates a string followed by a space, followed by an integer with a maximum field width of two, followed by a space and then a single character, followed by a newline.

```
fprintf (list, "\nAverage age of boys : %.1f\n",
    average_boys_age) ;
```

Here, the output is a newline followed by the text string, followed by the boys' average age given to one decimal place, followed by a newline.

Exercises

1. What would the following comparisons yield, true or false?
   (i)   ('3' <= '5')
   (ii) ('7' > '9')
   (iii) ('B' < 'D')
   (iv) ('Z' <= 'T')
   (v)   ('+' > '!')
   (vi) ('A' == 'a')
2. Refer to the program in Fig. 8.2, then answer the following questions.
   (i) Could the else...if line of the program be replaced simply by else? State your reasoning.
   (ii) Given an input stream of AB   ?1X4   5+E; what would the output look like?
3. Refer to the program in Fig. 8.3 and its explanation in the text, then answer the following questions.
   (i) Why is the line #include <string.h> included in the program?
   (ii) What would happen if the input data included a line with five Z's, a space and then five X's?

(iii) What changes would need to be made if three strings were to be read at a time and reported on in a similar way?

4. An input file (EX0804.DAT) contains a coded message in the form of a list of letters and spaces terminated by an end marker of 9 or 8. It is required to decode the message by writing every fourth character to the file MESSAGE.DAT and to display the original coded message on the screen.

Complete the program given in EX0804.C (see Fig. 8.5) to find out what the message is.

5. The file EX0805.DAT contains the results of a recent programming examination. In each line of the input file there is a name consisting of up to 12 characters followed by a space and then the mark. The last line contains 12 Z characters, followed by a space then a zero. It is required to produce a print file with headings at the top and the average mark and standard deviation at the foot of the list of student names and marks. It is also required to print FAIL alongside any mark that is less than 40.

Complete the program EX0805.C (see Fig. 8.6), then implement your work. Note, marksqrsum should be declared as type long because the size of this number may be outside the range for variables of type int.

6. The file EX0806.DAT contains the results of the football matches played on a certain Saturday. It is required to produce a program that displays on the screen the result of the game in which most goals have been scored. The format of the file is (on each line):

Home team name (up to 12 characters) followed by home team goals (an integer) followed by away team name (up to 12 characters) followed by away team goals (an integer).

The last line (end marker) of the file contains Zs in the team positions and zero in the goals positions. For example, the input

```
Manchester    4 Birmingham    4
Liverpool     7 Everton       5
Chelsea       1 Arsenal       5
ZZZZZZZZZZZZ  0 ZZZZZZZZZZZZ  0
```

would give the following results:

```
The result with the highest number of goals is:
Liverpool 7 Everton 5
```

Use the outline design in EX0806.C (see Fig. 8.7) to complete the production of this program.

```
/* To decode a message from ex0804.dat */
#include <stdio.h>
main ()
{
/* Description ......
   Open files                                              [cheat126]
   Initialize character position                           [cheat127]
   Read first character                                    [cheat128]
   WHILE not at the end of the file                        [cheat129]
      Display character on the screen                      [cheat130]
      IF current character position is a multiple of 4 [cheat131]
         Write to message file
      Increase character position by 1                     [cheat132]
      Read next character                                  [cheat133]
   Close files                                             [cheat134]
*/

   int charpos ;           /* current character position */
/* Other variables as needed                       [cheat135] */

}
```

Figure 8.5

```
/* Program to produce the exam list for programming */
#include <stdio.h>
#include <string.h>
#include <math.h>
main ()
{
/* Description ......
   Ready files and read first line                [cheat136]
   Initialize counts                              [cheat137]
   Write heading line                             [cheat138]
   WHILE not at the end of the file               [cheat139]
      Write name and mark                         [cheat140]
      IF mark < 40                                [cheat141]
         Write 'FAIL'
      ELSE
         Write end of line
      Add mark to sum of marks                    [cheat142]
      Add mark squared to sum of marks squared [cheat143]
      Add one to student count                    [cheat144]
      Read next line                              [cheat145]
   IF number of students not zero                 [cheat146]
      Compute average and standard deviation      [cheat147]
      ( note: standard deviation is given by:
      sqrt ((marksqrsum / student count) - pow (average, 2))
      Write average and standard deviation        [cheat148]
   Close files                                    [cheat149]
*/

   char name [13] ;            /* name of student */
/* Other variables as required                [cheat150] */

}
```

Figure 8.6

```
/* Program to find highest scoring game */
#include <stdio.h>
#include <string.h>
main ()
{
/* Description ......
   Ready input file and read first result              [cheat173]
   Initialize highest score = -1                       [cheat174]
   WHILE not end of results file                       [cheat175]
      IF total goals > highest so far                  [cheat176]
         Store teams and goals, update highest score   [cheat177]
      Read next result                                 [cheat178]
   Display highest result                              [cheat179]
   Close input file                                    [cheat180]
*/

/* Variables as required                               [cheat181] */


}
```

Figure 8.7

9

More control statements

9.1 The `for` statement

There is a significant difference between processing an iteration when we know in advance the number of times we will go round the loop and when we do not know the number of times in advance. The former, as we have already seen, are determinate, for example, when we know we are to process 24 items. The latter are indeterminate, for example, when we want to process a list of arbitrary length, ending with a particular end marker.

To use determinate loops we need to know in advance of entering the loop the number of iterations. Typically we have a count to control the number of iterations, hence the expression *count-controlled repetition*. Obviously, a count-controlled loop must have:

- A counter (called a control variable)
- A value at the start of the loop (initial value)
- A value that terminates the loop (final value)
- A value to add to the counter (increment)

The loop is then performed several times with the counter taking on the following values at each iteration:

```
First iteration:   initial value
Second iteration: initial value + increment
Third iteration:   initial value + increment + increment
          . . .
Last iteration:    final value.
```

That is, the control variable proceeds from initial value to final value in equal steps given by the increment.

C provides a special construct, the for statement, with which we can construct determinate loops. Actually, it is much more powerful than simply a count-controlled loop mechanism, but in its basic form it is a convenient way to implement such loops. Let us consider a simple example of using the for statement for count-controlled loops:

```
for (counter = 1 ; counter <= 3 ; ++ counter)
    printf ("%d\n", counter) ;
```

The effect of this loop is to display the numbers 1 to 3 on successive lines. Notice that the for statement has the keyword for followed by three expressions, separated by semicolons and enclosed in parentheses. The first expression is, in effect, a loop initialization (the control variable, counter, is given the initial value). The second is the condition that must remain true for the loop to be continued (this specifies the final value). The third is an expression that will be executed at the end of the loop every time the loop is executed (in this case the increment of 1 is added to counter). We can trace this action through for the above example:

counter is given a value of 1 (first expression)

counter <= 3 is true (second expression)
content of counter (1) is displayed (loop statement)
counter is incremented by 1 to 2 (third expression)

counter <= 3 is true (second expression)
content of counter (2) is displayed (loop statement)
counter is incremented by 1 to 3 (third expression)

counter <= 3 is true (second expression)
content of counter (3) is displayed (loop statement)
counter is incremented by 1 to 4 (third expression)

counter <= 3 is false (second expression)
the loop is complete and control is passed to the next statement.

Consider the program fragment given in Fig. 9.1.

The printf statement will be executed four times using values of 5, 6, 7 and 8 for kvalue. The first time round the loop, tvalue will have the same value as kvalue because it has been initialized to zero and kvalue (5) is added to it. The second time round the loop, tvalue will have the second value of kvalue added to it; the third time, the third value of kvalue is added, and the final time the fourth value of kvalue is added to it. Hence the output will be:

```
5  5
6  11
7  18
8  26
```

```
tvalue = 0 ;
for (kvalue = 5 ; kvalue <= 8 ; ++ kvalue)
    {
    tvalue = tvalue + kvalue ;
    printf ("%d %d\n", kvalue, tvalue) ;
    }
```

Figure 9.1

```
tvalue = 0 ;
kvalue = 5 ;
while (kvalue <= 8)
    {
    tvalue = tvalue + kvalue ;
    printf ("%d %d\n", kvalue, tvalue) ;
    ++ kvalue ;
    }
```

Figure 9.2

We can illustrate the for statement by comparing it with a while statement. Figure 9.2 shows the equivalent code to that in Fig. 9.1, but using the while statement.

Notice where the three expressions from the for statement appear in this piece of code. The general for statement,

```
for (expression-1 ; expression-2 ; expression-3)
    statement ;
```

can be written as

```
expression-1 ;
while (expression-2)
    {
    statement ;
    expression-3 ;
    }
```

The fact that a for statement may be written in the form of a while statement implies that the for statement is redundant. However, the for statement does convey to the human reader in one line everything that controls the loop, and should now be used for count-controlled loops.

As we have already illustrated with the if...else and while statements, any control statement can be nested within any other control statement. The program given as Fig. 9.3 demonstrates nested for loops. You should examine it and determine its output.

```
/* Outputs number pairs using nested for loops */
#include <stdio.h>
main ()
{
/* Description ......
    FOR all values in outer loop range
        FOR all values in inner loop range
            Output current pair of numbers
*/
    const int outer_initial = 10,
              outer_final = 13,
              inner_initial = 100,
              inner_final = 102 ;

    int outer_counter,
        inner_counter ;

    for (outer_counter = outer_initial ; outer_counter <=
        outer_final ; ++ outer_counter)
        for (inner_counter = inner_initial ; inner_counter <=
            inner_final ; ++ inner_counter)
            printf ("%3d %3d\n", outer_counter, inner_counter) ;
}
```

Figure 9.3

9.2   The `do-while` statement

The do statement is another loop control statement. Unlike the while and for statements, it tests for another repetition at the bottom of the loop instead of the top. For example,

```
do
    scanf ("%d", number) ;
while (number <= 20) ;
printf ("%d\n", number) ;
```

will read integers until a number greater than 20 is read, when the loop will stop and the printf statement will be obeyed. The sequence of operations is:

1. Obey the statement between do and while.
2. Test the condition. If it is true, repeat from the above step.
3. If it is false, continue with the rest of the program.

As with while and for, several statements enclosed in braces may be placed inside the loop.

Let us compare the while loop with the do-while loop.

```
while
```

1. The condition is tested before each repetition of the loop.
2. The number of repetitions can be zero or more.

```
do-while
```

1. The condition is tested after each repetition of the loop.
2. The number of repetitions must be at least one.

It can be argued that this difference is insufficient to justify the two distinct constructs. However, the do statement does make explicit the fact that the loop is always executed at least once. It should be used when the loop has to be executed once before the condition can be tested. This may be illustrated by an example. Consider the following interactive dialogue where user input is indicated by underlining:

```
Enter number to be squared: 5
The square is 25
Do you want to continue (Y or N)? Y

Enter number to be squared: 12
The square is 144
Do you want to continue (Y or N)? Y

Enter number to be squared: 11
The square is 121
Do you want to continue (Y or N)? N

Exit
```

The condition for continuing, while (user_response == 'Y'), can only be evaluated once the user has entered Y or N. This occurs at the end of the first execution of the loop. The complete program is given in Fig. 9.4.

9.3   The `switch` statement

Consider the following program fragment that displays a number as text depending on the value contained in the char variable character.

```
if (character == 'I')
   printf ("1\n") ;
else if (character == 'V')
   printf ("5\n") ;
else if (character == 'X')
   printf ("10\n") ;
else if (character == 'L')
   printf ("50\n") ;
else
   printf ("Not a Roman numeral\n") ;
```

```
/* A program to demonstrate do while */
#include <stdio.h>
main ()
{
/* Description   ......
    DO
        Prompt for and accept number
        Display square of number
        Prompt for and accept user continue response
    WHILE user continue response is Y
    Display 'Exit'
*/
    char user_response ;
    int  number ;

    do
        {
        printf ("Enter number to be squared: ") ;
        scanf ("%d", &number) ;
        printf ("The square is %d\n", number * number) ;
        printf ("Do you want to continue (Y or N)? ") ;
        scanf ("\n%c", &user_response) ;
        printf ("\n") ;
        }
    while (user_response == 'Y') ;
    printf ("Exit\n") ;
}
```

Figure 9.4

This is an example of a situation where we want the program to select one of several different courses of action depending on the value of a single variable, in this case the variable character. With more than three or four courses of action the above approach could become rather clumsy.

What we need is a means by which the desired course of action is selected immediately after a single inspection of the value of the variable. C provides the switch statement. Using switch we can code the above as follows:

```
switch (character)
    {
    case 'I'  : printf ("1\n") ;
                break ;
    case 'V'  : printf ("5\n") ;
                break ;
    case 'X'  : printf ("10\n") ;
                break ;
    case 'L'  : printf ("50\n") ;
                break ;
```

```
default    : printf ("Not a Roman numeral\n") ;
}
```

Following the keyword switch, we have a controlling expression in parentheses that must give an integer value or, as above, a character value. In our case it is the single char variable character. There follows, enclosed within braces, any number of case groups. A case group consists of the keyword case followed by a possible value of the controlling expression, followed by a colon, followed by a statement to be executed if the controlling expression has the specified value, followed by the break statement. The break statement is optional. It exists to prevent the execution 'falling through' to the following statements belonging to other cases. Optionally, as above, the case groups may be followed by a default group that specifies a statement to be executed if the controlling expression contains a value not matched in any of the case groups.

The effect of a switch statement is as follows:

1. The controlling expression is evaluated.
2. One case-labelled statement is obeyed, namely the statement that is labelled by the controlling expression's value.
3. If the controlling expression gives a value that is not labelled by a case, the statement following default is obeyed (if it is present).

The controlling expression must evaluate to an integer result (int) or be of type char, and the case labels must all be distinct constants of the same type.

Several constants may be placed in front of the same labelled statements. This is used when the same action is to be taken for several different selected values. For example, we could have:

```
case 4   :
case 7   :
case 15  : counter += 2 ;
           break ;
```

If several actions are required from the same case group, we can write several statements following the colon. For example,

```
case 25  : premium_rate = 0.95 ;
           printf ("Discount allowed\n") ;
           break ;
```

Potential values must occur once only as case labels. The following example is incorrect:

```
switch (value / price)
   {
   case 1 :
   case 3 : printf ("1 or 3\n") ;
```

```
            break ;
    case 3 :
    case 4 : printf ("3 or 4\n") ;
            break ;
    }
```

To ensure that you understand the effects of the switch statement, you should examine the program given in Fig. 9.5 (see Exercise 2).

Exercises

1. Demonstrate your understanding of for by rewriting the program in Fig. 9.3 without using for statements.
2. What output would be given from the program in Fig. 9.5 when used with the following input cases?
   (i)   7 2
   (ii) 1 6
   (iii) 2 7
   (iv) 1 1
   (v) 1 8
   (vi) −1 6
3. Using the outline design in EX0903.C (see Fig. 9.6), code and test a program to prompt Which times table do you require?, then read the integer value (n say) supplied by the user and then output the n-times table in the form:

```
 1 x n = 999
 2 x n = 999
 .  .  .   .  .  .
12 x n = 999
```

4. Using the outline design in EX0904.C (see Fig. 9.7), code and test a program that accepts as input two integers that represent the depth and width of a box. You may assume that the depth will be not greater than 23 and the width not greater than 79. The program is to display a box on the screen outlined by the appropriate number of X's. You should assume that the minimum size will be 3 x 3. For example, 6 5 would give:

```
XXXXX
X   X
X   X
X   X
X   X
XXXXX
```

The code for the top line requires one for statement and is identical to that for the bottom line. You are advised to code 'process middle lines' using nested `for` statements.

5. From the outline design in EX0905.C (see Fig. 9.8), write an interactive program that prompts for, and reads, two integer values representing a month and a year between 1910 and 1990 inclusive. For each pair of values the program determines the number of days in that month (allowing for leap years) using the `switch` statement. The program should continue displaying the result with appropriate text until negative values are input to signify no more calculations. You may find it useful to draw a sample dialogue.

6. Code and test a program (using the outline design in EX0906.C and referring to Fig. 9.9) that will accept simple integer arithmetic statements and produce the correct answer. The statements will be of the form: operand operator operand. A sample dialogue with user input shown underlined might be

```
Enter statement, (e.g. 63 + 25) : 53 - 42
53 - 42 = 11
Do you wish to continue? - answer Y or N Y
Enter statement, (e.g. 63 + 25) : 55 * 6
55 * 6 = 330
Do you wish to continue? - answer Y or N Y
Enter statement, (e.g. 63 + 25) : 99 / 33
99 / 33 = 3
Do you wish to continue? - answer Y or N N
```

7. A text file contains a line with one integer value representing the number of lines that follow. These lines contain first an integer value representing the number of items that follow on that line. Each item consists of an integer followed by a character; the integer is a length measurement, the character is one of C, M, I or Y – to indicate centimetres, metres, inches or yards.

For example, we might have a file as follows:

```
3
2 10 C 12 I
3 2 Y 5 C 2 M
4 3 M 4 C 25 C 2 I
```

It is required to produce output in standard form, that is, in CMS. Given the above input we would produce an output file as follows:

```
            LENGTH CONVERSION
Line 1 :
    Item  1 :    10 CMS =    10.00 CMS
    Item  2 :    12 INS =    30.48 CMS
Total for line 1       =    40.48 CMS
```

```
Line 2 :
   Item  1 :      2 YDS =   182.88 CMS
   Item  2 :      5 CMS =     5.00 CMS
   Item  3 :      2 MTS =   200.00 CMS
Total for line 2       =   387.88 CMS
Line 3 :
   Item  1 :      3 MTS =   300.00 CMS
   Item  2 :      4 CMS =     4.00 CMS
   Item  3 :     25 CMS =    25.00 CMS
   Item  4 :      2 INS =     5.08 CMS
Total for line 3       =   334.08 CMS
```

Use the outline design in EX0907.C and refer to Fig. 9.10 to code and test the program that will accomplish this. You should use the switch statement to examine a unit of measurement with each case-labelled statement making the appropriate conversion.

```
/* Illustrates the switch statement */
#include <stdio.h>
main ()
{
/* Description  ......
   Read two integers
   Examine second integer using switch
*/
   int  group,
        intone,
        inttwo ;

   printf ("Enter two integers : ") ;
   scanf ("%d%d", &intone, &inttwo) ;
   group = 0 ;
   switch (inttwo)
      {
      case 1 :
      case 4 :
         group = 1 ;
         printf ("%d\n", intone) ;
         break ;
      case 6 :
         if (intone < 1)
             printf ("%d\n", intone) ;
         else
             printf ("%d\n", inttwo) ;
         break ;
      case 7 :
         group = 3 ;
         break ;
      default :
         group = 4 ;
      }
   printf ("Group is %d\n", group) ;
}
```

Figure 9.5

```
/* Reads an integer and outputs the N times table */
#include <stdio.h>
main ()
{
/* Description ......
   Prompt for and read N                      [cheat196]
   FOR multiplier from 1 to 12 in steps of 1 [cheat197]
      Display multiplier * N line
*/

/* Constants as necessary                     [cheat198] */

/* Variables as necessary                     [cheat199] */


}
```

Figure 9.6

```
/* To display a box of max. dimensions 23 X 79 */
#include <stdio.h>
main ()
{
/* Description ......
   Prompt for and read dimensions      [cheat206]
   Process top line                    [cheat207]
   Process middle lines                [cheat208]
   Process bottom line                 [cheat209]
*/

/* Variables as necessary              [cheat210] */



}
```

Figure 9.7

```
/* Displays the number of days for a given month */
#include <stdio.h>
main ()
{
/* Description ......
   Prompt for and get month and year         [cheat211]
   WHILE user requires output                [cheat212]
      Determine no. of days in month         [cheat213]
      Display result                         [cheat214]
      Prompt for and get next month and year [cheat215]
*/

/* Variables as required                     [cheat216] */



}
```

Figure 9.8

```
/* Allows simple arithmetic statements to be interpreted */
#include <stdio.h>
main ()
{
/* Description ......
   DO                                    [cheat218]
      Prompt for and read input          [cheat219]
      Evaluate and execute operation     [cheat220]
      Accept continue response           [cheat221]
   WHILE user wants to continue          [cheat222]
*/

/* Variables as required                 [cheat223] */


}
```

Figure 9.9

```
/* Reads file of measurements and converts to standard cms. */
#include <stdio.h>
main ()
{
/* Description ......
   Prepare files and get number of lines              [cheat224]
   Output result headings                             [cheat225]
   FOR each line in turn                              [cheat226]
      Output line subheading                          [cheat227]
      Read number of items                            [cheat228]
      Initialize line total                           [cheat229]
      FOR each item in a line                         [cheat230]
         Read item length and unit of measurement     [cheat231]
         Examine unit of measurement and make conversion [cheat232]
         Output item details                          [cheat233]
         Accumulate line total                        [cheat234]
      Output line total                               [cheat235]
   Close files                                        [cheat236]
*/
   const float cms_per_metre = 100,
               cms_per_inch = 2.54,
               cms_per_yard = 91.44 ;

/* Any necessary variables                            [cheat237] */

}
```

Figure 9.10

10

Functions

10.1   The function call

We have already used many functions such as `printf`, `scanf` and `sqrt` which are provided by C in standard libraries. We have noted the benefits of being able to write

```
period = 2 * pi * sqrt (pendulum / gravity) ;
```

and

```
printf ("%5.2f %d", real_number, int_number) ;
```

without having to write the code to evaluate the square root or provide the necessary conversions when outputting numbers. When using such functions, we say that the function is called or invoked.

The expressions in parentheses following the function's name are the arguments of the function. Each argument is an expression of a type appropriate to the function.

A C program may consist of the main program function and any number of subprograms called functions. A function is a self-contained subprogram that can be called (invoked) from a main program or another subprogram.

We shall now use some of the library functions that we have already met to illustrate the most common ways in which functions are called in C.

10.1.1 A FUNCTION CALL AS PART OF AN EXPRESSION

This use of a function can be illustrated by the following examples.

The function sqrt, found in <math.h>, takes a single argument and returns a result of type double (double is an extended form of type float). For example,

```
period = 2 * pi * sqrt (pendulum_length / gravity) ;
```

The function pow on the other hand takes two arguments and returns a result of type double. For example,

```
second_number_cubed = pow (second_number, 3) ;
```

The function strcmp, found in <string.h>, takes two arguments and returns a single result of type int. For example,

```
if (strcmp (first_string, "ZZZZZ") == 0)
```

The arguments and result types of these functions may differ, but the functions all have one important characteristic. The function call has a single value and appears in an expression, normally on the right-hand side of an assignment statement or in a conditional expression. Notice also that the arguments are supplied to the function but are not changed by the function; for example, second_number has the same value after the function pow has been called as it had before.

10.1.2 A FUNCTION CALL AS A PROGRAM STATEMENT WHEN ITS ARGUMENTS ARE NOT CHANGED BY THE FUNCTION

This situation can be illustrated by

```
printf ("%3d %3d\n", outer_counter, inner_counter) ;
```

In this case, the function call is not used within an expression. It is an executable statement that uses the arguments to achieve a specific objective. The values of the arguments are not changed by the function call. (Notice that printf is unusual in that the number and type of its arguments are not predetermined, but can vary.)

10.1.3 A FUNCTION CALL AS A PROGRAM STATEMENT WHEN SOME OR ALL OF ITS ARGUMENTS ARE CHANGED BY THE FUNCTION

Now consider a situation that can be typified by the following example.

```
strcpy (symbol_2, symbol_1) ;
```

The string held in symbol_1 is copied into symbol_2. Thus, one argument (symbol_1) is supplied to the function and does not have its value changed by the function. The other argument (symbol_2) does have its value changed as a result of the function call.
Similarly, in

```
fscanf (classfile, "%c%d%s", &sex, &age, name) ;
```

the last three arguments will have new values after the function call.

Again the function call is not used within an expression, but as an executable statement. It differs from the situations in Section 10.1.2 in that some (or all) of the arguments may have their values changed as a result of the function call.

You should note that, although we have categorized functions into three general areas above, C allows for all functions to return a result value as well as the possibility of having arguments whose values may or may not be changed.

The C programs we have seen so far are themselves functions. Recall that we start the executable part of our program with main (), which is a function heading with no result type specified and an empty parameter list.

10.2 The function definition

We cannot expect a programming language to anticipate every conceivable need for a function, so we need a facility by which the programmer can define the functions we require.

This facility is called the *function definition*. It has the following general form:

```
result_type function_name (parameter list)
{
    declarations
    statements
}
```

Let us consider a function definition within a program by examining the program in Fig. 10.1.

After the start of the program we have two declarations:

```
int number ;
int cube (int) ;
```

The first is a declaration for the variable identifier number of type int. The second is a *function prototype*. It informs the compiler that there will be a function called cube that has one argument of type int and delivers a result of type int.

The function definition for cube is

```
int cube (int item)
{
    return item * item * item ;
}
```

We will use the convention of placing our function definitions after the main program code. The first line of the function definition is the *function header*. It contains the *result type* int, followed by the *function name* cube, followed by the *parameter list* in parentheses. In this case, the parameter list contains only one entry defining an integer parameter called item. We refer to item as a *formal*

```
/* Sample program to demonstrate a function */
#include <stdio.h>
main ()
{
    int number ;
    int cube (int) ;

    number = cube (3) ;
    printf ("3 cubed is %d\n", number) ;
}

/* Function to return parameter cubed */
int cube (int item)
{
    return item * item * item ;
}
```

Figure 10.1

parameter. Notice that the header matches the prototype in terms of the result type, function name and number and type of arguments.

The code in braces is referred to as the *body* of the function. In this case it consists of a single `return` statement. The `return` statement is not mandatory, but it must be included with an expression following it when the corresponding function call yields a single value as part of an expression. The value of the expression following the keyword `return` is returned. In our case above, the value of `item` is multiplied by itself twice, giving $item^3$, and it is this value that is returned.

Since `cube` has just one integer formal parameter, it must be invoked by a function call containing just one integer expression as its argument. For example,

```
number = cube (3) ;
```

This statement contains a function call to the function `cube` with the argument 3. The integer result, in this case 27, will be assigned to the integer variable `number`.

Having included the above definition in a program, we could also write:

```
printf ("%d", cube (numbera + numberb)) ;
```

or

```
funny_number = sqrt (cube (number_one * number_two)) ;
```

Whenever the function is called, the values of the arguments are assigned to (substituted for) the corresponding formal parameter. If an argument is an expression, it is evaluated and the resultant value is passed to the function.

The power of this facility lies in the fact that having defined a function we can then use it with different arguments at different stages of a program.

Function definitions are not restricted to one statement. More usually, several statements are needed to work out the result and these statements may require identifiers of their own, identifiers which are of no concern to the rest of the program. C allows a function to have its own internal declaration part; this enables us to define local identifiers for the function. Hence the function declaration resembles a complete program. For this reason it is called a *subprogram*.

Let us now study the example program given as Fig. 10.2.

The stages involved when a function is called are now described with respect to the program in Fig. 10.2. Suppose the user enters the values 2 and 5 for `firsta` and `lasta`. Let us consider the first function call, `sum_of_sqrs` `(firsta, lasta)`.

1. The arguments `firsta` and `lasta` are paired off with the formal parameters `first` and `last` in the function definition.
2. A store location is created for each formal parameter of the function, to which is assigned the value of the corresponding argument.

   `first [ 2 ]          last [ 5 ]`

3. A store location is created for each local variable of the function. The value of `number` is undefined.

   `number [ ? ]          sum [ 0 ]`

4. The function's statements are executed, resulting in:

   `number [ 6 ]          sum [ 54 ]`
   `returned value [ 54 ]`

5. All store locations created for the formal parameters and for the local variables are discarded. The value of the function result is used as the value of the function call, that is, `sum_of_sqrs` `(firsta,   lasta)` assumes the value 54.

Obviously the above process would be performed at each call, so in our program it would then be repeated with the values entered for `firstb` and `lastb`.

We can see a direct, one-for-one relationship between the parameters defined as part of a function heading and the arguments passed to the function when it is called. We also see that the values of the arguments are assigned to the corresponding formal parameters. If an argument is an expression, it is evaluated and the resultant value is passed to the function.

It should be noted that both of the user-defined functions considered in this section, `cube` and `sum_of_sqrs`, are examples of the situation where the function call yields a single value and is used as part of an expression.

```
/* A program to compare the sum of squares between two */
/* different ranges of numbers                         */
#include <stdio.h>
main ()
{
/* Description ...... 
   Prompt for and read first range
   Prompt for and read second range
   Compare sum of squares and display message
*/
   int firsta,
       lasta,                 /* first range */
       firstb,
       lastb ;                /* second range */
   int sum_of_sqrs (int, int) ;

   printf ("Enter first range : ") ;
   scanf ("%d%d", &firsta, &lasta) ;
   printf ("Enter second range: ") ;
   scanf ("%d%d", &firstb, &lastb) ;
   if (sum_of_sqrs (firsta, lasta) > sum_of_sqrs (firstb, lastb))
      printf ("First sum of squares > second\n") ;
   else
      printf ("First sum of squares < second\n") ;
}

/* Returns sum of squares between first and last */
#include <math.h>
int sum_of_sqrs (int first, int last)
{
/* Description ...... 
   Initialize sum to zero
   FOR each number in the range
      Accumulate number squared
   Return sum of squares
*/
   int number,
       sum = 0 ;

   for (number = first ; number <= last ; ++ number)
      sum += pow (number, 2) ;
   return sum ;
}
```

Figure 10.2

10.3   Function parameters and arguments

As we saw in Section 10.1, a function call can be a program statement, in which case it does not have a value and the result type is said to be void. The function call

```
/* Function to display a screen heading */
void display_heading (int screen_no)
{
/* Description ......
   Display screen heading
   Display screen number
*/
   printf ("          Personnel Report Screen\n") ;
   printf ("Screen number %d\n\n", screen_no) ;
}
```

Figure 10.3

```
display_heading (screen_count) ;
```

would have a function prototype of the form

```
void display_heading (int) ;
```

and a function definition of the form given in Fig. 10.3. Notice that in this case there is no need to include a `return` statement.

A function does not necessarily have to have parameters. The parameters are then said to be void. We would have a function call of the form

```
initialize () ;
```

with a function prototype and definition heading of the form

```
void initialize (void)
```

or

```
void initialize ()
```

A common reason for using functions without parameters is simply to break up a program into smaller components either to facilitate design or coding. We shall use one of our previous examples to demonstrate a simple program using functions without parameters. This program is shown in Fig. 10.4.

Notice that the variable declarations have been included before `main ()`. This allows the main program function and all of the subprogram functions access to the variables, which are then said to be *global* in scope.

There still remains the problem of how to define and use a function that can be called as a program statement and will then change the values of some of the arguments. The situation was illustrated by `strcpy` and `scanf` in Section 10.1.

The answer to this lies in the way in which we specify the arguments and parameters to such functions. Recall that in `scanf` we placed a `&` before the variables into which we required data. This is the way we indicate the *address* (or place in computer storage) of a value held by a variable. When we specify the address of a variable in this way we allow its value to be changed by the function.

```
/* Counts the capital letters and digits in an input file */
#include <stdio.h>
   int  letter_count,
        digit_count ;
   char character ;
   FILE *inpfile,
        *outpfile ;

main ()
{
/* Description  ......
   Initialization and read first character
   WHILE not end of input file
      Process a character and read next one
   Output results
   Close files
*/
   void initialize () ;
   void process_character () ;
   void output_results () ;

   initialize () ;
   while (! ((character == ';') || (character == '.')))
      process_character () ;
   output_results () ;
   fclose (inpfile) ;
   fclose (outpfile) ;
}

/* Function for initialization and read first character */
void initialize ()
{
/* Description  ......
   Open files
   Initialize counts
   Read first character
*/
   inpfile = fopen ("inpfile.dat", "r") ;
   outpfile = fopen ("outpfile.dat", "w") ;
   letter_count = 0 ;
   digit_count = 0 ;
   fscanf (inpfile, "%c", &character) ;
}
   /* Function to process a character and read the next one */
   void process_character ()
   {
   /* Description  ......
      Write the current character
      Add to appropriate ccunt
      Read the next character
   */
```

Figure 10.4

```
      fprintf (outpfile, "%c", character) ;
      if ((character >= 'A') && (character <= 'Z'))
         letter_count += 1 ;
      else if ((character >= '0') && (character <= '9'))
         digit_count += 1 ;
      fscanf (inpfile, "%c", &character) ;
}

/* Function to output results */
void output_results ()
{
/* Description  ...... 
   Output the letter count
   Output the digit count
*/
      fprintf (outpfile, "\nThere are %d capital letters",
         letter_count) ;
      fprintf (outpfile, " and %d digits", digit_count) ;
}
```

Figure 10.4   Continued.

It is important to understand the difference between a variable name and an address. Since the address is a location in computer storage, it can be visualized as pointing to the location as shown in Fig. 10.5.

Figure 10.5

The variable `variable_name` holds the value 20 at the location given by (address) in memory.

Consider the example given as Fig. 10.6. First notice the function prototype

```
void swap (float *, float *) ;
```

The keyword `void` indicates that there will be no value returned as the result of the function named `swap`. The parameters of the function demonstrate a feature of C that we have not yet met, the indirection operator *. We use the indirection operator to denote the address of a location in the computer's memory. In this case, we are saying that the arguments and parameters of `swap` will be the addresses of two `float` variables.

```
/* Orders each of a number of data pairs */
#include <stdio.h>
main ()
{
/* Description ...... 
   Prompt for and read number of pairs
   FOR all data pairs
       Prompt for and read a pair of numbers
       Swap if necessary
       Output the ordered pair
*/
   float first_number,
         second_number ;
   int   counter,
         number_of_pairs ;
   void  swap (float *, float *) ;

   printf ("Enter number of pairs ") ;
   scanf ("%d", &number_of_pairs) ;
   for (counter = 1 ; counter <= number_of_pairs ; ++ counter)
       {
       printf ("Enter a data pair ") ;
       scanf ("%f%f", &first_number, &second_number) ;
       if (first_number > second_number)
           swap (&first_number, &second_number) ;
       printf ("In order - %.2f %.2f\n", first_number,
           second_number) ;
       }
}

/* Function to swap contents of two variables */
void swap (float *first, float *second)
{
/* Description ...... 
   Swap contents of variables
*/
   float temp ;          /* temporary area */

   temp = *first ;
   *first = *second ;
   *second = temp ;
}
```

Figure 10.6

```
swap (&first_number, &second_number) ;
```

is the function call to swap. The two arguments are the addresses of the two
float variables first_number and second_number.

Now we will consider the function definition.

```
void swap (float *first, float *second)
```

As we have already seen in the prototype, there is to be no value returned as the function result; we use the keyword void. The formal parameters, *first and *second, will contain the address of variables of type float.

```
float temp ;
```

We need to declare a variable to hold one of the two values temporarily so that we can effect the swap. This is needed only within the function, so we declare it as part of the function.

```
temp = *first ;
*first = *second ;
*second = temp ;
```

Here we have three assignment statements that are understood as follows:

1. temp is assigned the value of the variable whose address is contained in first.
2. The variable whose address is contained in first is assigned the value of the variable whose address is contained in second.
3. The variable whose address is contained in second is assigned the value of temp.

We use the operators & and * in association with each other. The & operators in the function call argument list match the * operators in the function header parameters. In the assignment statements, instead of referring to the parameters directly by name, we do so indirectly through their addresses. Hence if the formal parameter has the * operator, then when it is used in the body of the function it must also be preceded by *.

To demonstrate how the values of the arguments are changed, it is useful to consider the computer storage locations. Suppose the first pair of values to be entered is 9 and 7.

1. When swap (&first_number, &second_number) is called, the addresses of first_number and second_number are used in the formal parameters such that *first points to first_number and *second points to second_number. We can visualize this as shown in Fig. 10.7.

2. We can now trace what happens as the function is executed:

	first_number	second_number	temp
	9	7	?
temp = *first			9
*first = *second	7		
*second = temp		9	

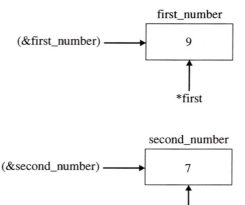

Figure 10.7

Figure 10.8

3. Upon completion, the variable `temp` is discarded and the variables `first_number` and `second_number` have had their values changed to those shown in Fig. 10.8.

The difference between the mechanism outlined here (known as simulated call by reference) and that described in Section 10.2 for the arguments of `sum_of_sqrs` (known as call by value) can be summarized as follows:

1. Call by value:
   (i)   A store location is created for the formal parameter.
   (ii) The value of the argument is then assigned to this location.
   (iii) When the function statements are executed, the value in the location for the formal parameter is used.
   (iv) Consequently, the argument is not changed and is used only to supply a value to the function.

2. Simulated call by reference:
   (i)   A store location is created to hold an address for the formal parameter.
   (ii) The address of the argument is then assigned to this location.

```
/* Sample program to illustrate C scope rules */
#include <stdio.h>
   char global = 'F' ;
   FILE *listfile ;

main ()
{
   char local_main = 'C' ;
   void print_word (int) ;

   listfile = fopen ("list.dat", "w") ;
   print_word (1) ;
   print_word (2) ;
   global = local_main ;
   print_word (3) ;
   fclose (listfile) ;
}

/* Function to print an integer and a word */
void print_word (int item)
{
   char local_print = 'H' ;

   fprintf (listfile, "%d %cat\n", item, global) ;
   global = local_print ;
}
```

Figure 10.9

   (iii) When the function is called, any operation involving the formal parameter
         is performed using the variable whose address is contained within the
         parameter.
   (iv) Consequently, the value of the variable whose address is the argument can
         be changed and is used to carry values out of the function.

A function could have some arguments using call by value and some using
simulated call by reference.

10.4   Scope

Normally, we can regard functions as so-called black boxes that perform precisely
the actions required of them as long as we provide any necessary pre-specified
arguments. We do not need to know how the function achieves its results. In
functions any local declarations are completely private; they may only be used
within the function that owns them. This even applies to the main program
function.

   We say that the scope of local declarations is limited to the local function body.
However, as we have seen in Fig. 10.4, there are circumstances when we wish to
have declarations of global scope, that is, declarations that can be used by any

function in the program file. Let us consider the program in Fig. 10.9, and explain why it will output

```
1 Fat
2 Hat
3 Cat
```

After the include statement we have a global declaration with an initial value of F:

```
char global = 'F' ;
```

The variable global is now available to both of the functions in the program file. Similarly, the output file pointer must be declared here as it is referred to in the main program and the subprogram. The next declaration is after the main header:

```
char local_main = 'C' ;
```

This variable is within the body of main () and so has local scope to main (). It is followed by:

```
void print_word (int) ;
```

which is the function prototype for print_word. This function prints the integer argument followed by the character contained in the global variable global followed by the characters at. Next we have a call to this function:

```
print_word (1) ;
```

This will cause 1 Fat to be printed. It is followed by another call to the function but with a different result:

```
print_word (2) ;
```

This time 2 Hat will be printed because the first time that print_word was called, the variable global was changed from its initial value of F to H (the content of the local variable local_print). Next comes an assignment:

```
global = local_main ;
```

This will change the variable global from H to C. Then when the next call is made to the function we get another different result:

```
print_word (3) ;
```

This time 3 Cat will be printed.

Now for a brief explanation of the function. First the header:

```
void print_word (int item)
```

This shows that the function does not return a value and has one parameter of type int. In the body of the function we have one local variable declaration:

```
char local_print = 'H' ;
```

This is accessible only in the function `print_word`. Finally the executable part of the function is

```
fprintf (listfile, "%d %cat\n", item, global) ;
global = local_print ;
```

This will, as has already been explained, print the parameter's value, followed by the contents of the global variable `global`, followed by the characters `at`. Then it will change the value of `global` to H.

10.5   Program development using functions

Let us now summarize the main advantages of adopting a program development strategy that involves using functions as building blocks for writing programs.

1. The program can be built from small (that is, manageable) self-contained subprograms. This often helps the design process by enabling the designer to consider the parts of a system separately.
2. Each function can be written and tested separately. This facilitates the development and testing of a large program, because testing a small unit is less complex than testing a large software unit.
3. Each function can be read and understood separately. The top levels of design (possibly the main program) may be more easily understood as a small number of function statements. Each function statement may be read without delving into the details of each function.
4. Once declared, a function may be invoked at several places, with different arguments if required. This makes it unnecessary to write similar pieces of program several times, which would be tedious and error prone.
5. Taking point 4 further, subprograms of general utility can be used in more than one program or even deposited in libraries where they can be used by other programmers. This is similar to the use of standard functions in C.
6. Functions provide flexibility in the sense that one version of a function can easily be replaced by another. This results from the self-contained nature of subprograms.
7. We can economize on storage space by declaring each variable only in the function where it is actually needed. This way, variables will only take up storage space each time they are needed. In contrast, global variables will use storage for the complete execution of the program, even if the function that uses them is not invoked.

When developing programs using functions it is important to specify each function clearly by carefully considering the following:

1. Will the function call be used as part of an expression or as a program statement, and what is the type of the result, if any, delivered by the function?
2. What parameters are required, and should they be implemented as call by value

or simulated call by reference?

3. Which variables should have global scope and which should be local to the function?

Exercises

1. Refer to the program in Fig. 10.2, and identify the following:
   (i)   The local identifiers of the function sum_of_sqrs.
   (ii) The formal parameters of the function sum_of_sqrs.
   (iii) The arguments of the function calls.
   Why is the variable sum necessary?
2. Given the following function definitions:

```
void swapa (int *param_x, int *param_y)
{
    int temp ;

    temp = *param_x ;
    *param_x = *param_y ;
    *param_y = temp ;
}

void swapb (int param_x, int param_y)
{
    int temp ;

    temp = param_x ;
    param_x = param_y ;
    param_y = temp ;
}
```

and assuming that argument_a has the value 4 and argument_b has the value 2, by considering the storage locations involved, explain what each of the following function calls achieves.

```
(1) swapa (&argument_a, &argument_b) ;
(2) swapb (argument_a, argument_b) ;
```

3. Prepare a simple program that accepts six integer values and is able to determine the maximum value using just one statement that uses function calls. The function max returns the larger of two integer numbers. The outline design and code for the main program is in EX1003.C and in Fig. 10.10.
4. The outline design in EX1004.C (see Fig. 10.11) is for a program that reads in a file of positive integers with an end marker of −1 and displays each integer on a separate line with the word MULTIPLE alongside if the integer is a multiple of 3 or 23 (or both). The program contains a function to detect numbers that are

such multiples.
5. EX1005.C and Fig. 10.12 contain the outline design for a program that evaluates

$$A^N - B^{2N}$$

The input file contains three numbers per line (A, B, N) where A and B are real and N is an integer. The end of the file is signified by N being −1. We will not use the pow function from the library, so a function has to be incorporated that will take two parameters, x and n, and evaluate x^n.
6. EX1006.C and Fig. 10.13 contain the outline design for an interactive program that allows the user to input ten lengths in metres, calls a function to convert each length to its imperial equivalent (feet and inches), and then displays the length in feet and inches. Complete the program and compile and test it in the usual way.
7. EX1007.C and Fig. 10.14 give the outline design for a program that obtains a date from the keyboard in the form of three integers representing the day, the month and the year respectively. The date is to be displayed in a standard form, for example the input 23 7 1993 would be displayed as 23/7/93. Then the date exactly six months from the input date is to be displayed, for example the same input date would give 23/1/94. In this exercise a complete function is to be written, including the heading.
8. Write a function to be used in processing a line of text comprising blanks followed by words of letters only. The function should skip the blanks and return the first and last letters of the word following the blanks.

   Hence incorporate the function in a program that outputs to the monitor screen a word formed by the first and last letters of the words in an input file (EX1008.DAT). The input file has as its terminator a word that has the same first and last letter and then a full stop.

   EX1008.C and Fig. 10.15 give the outline design for the main program and the function.

```
/* Program to find maximum of 6 integers using a function */
#include <stdio.h>
main ()
{
/* Description  ......
   Prompt for and read the 6 integers from the keyboard
   Display the maximum
*/
   int item1,
       item2,
       item3,
       item4,
       item5,
       item6 ;
   int max (int, int) ;

   printf ("Enter six integer values: ") ;
   scanf ("%d%d%d%d%d%d", &item1, &item2, &item3, &item4, &item5,
       &item6) ;
   printf ("The maximum is %d\n", max (max (max (max (max (item1,
       item2), item3), item4), item5), item6)) ;
}

/* Function to find the larger of two numbers */
int max (int first, int second)
{
/* Description  ......
   Returns greater of two integers - assumes not equal [cheat242]
*/


}
```

Figure 10.10

```
/* Program to determine which numbers from a file */
/* are multiples of 3 or 23 or both */
#include <stdio.h>
main ()
{
/* Description  ......
   Prepare input file and get first number            [cheat243]
   WHILE not end marker (-1)                           [cheat244]
      Display number and comment if appropriate        [cheat245]
      Get next number                                  [cheat246]
   Close the input file                                [cheat247]
*/
   int   input_number ;
   int   is_a_multiple (int) ;


}
```

Figure 10.11

```
/* Function find a multiple of 3 or 23 */
int is_a_multiple (int number)
{
/* Description  ......
   Returns a result of 0 if parameter is a multiple
      of 3 or 23 otherwise 1                      [cheat248]
*/
   int  result = 1 ;


}
```

Figure 10.11   Continued.

```
/* Program reads a file of triples (A, B, N) and evaluates */
/* A to the Nth - B to the 2Nth                            */
#include <stdio.h>
main ()
{
/* Description  ......
   Prepare input file                    [cheat249]
   Get first triple                      [cheat250]
   WHILE not end of file                 [cheat251]
      Calculate and display              [cheat252]
      Get next triple                    [cheat253]
   Close the input file                  [cheat254]
*/

/* Main program declarations            [cheat255] */


}

/* Function to return x to the power n calculated iteratively */
float power (float x, int n)
{
/* Description  ......
   Initialize multiple = 1.0             [cheat256]
   FOR counter from 1 to n               [cheat257]
      Multiply multiple by x             [cheat258]
   Return multiple                       [cheat259]
*/

/* Variables for function power          [cheat260] */


}
```

Figure 10.12

```
/* Reads in 10 lengths in metres and outputs the */
/* lengths in feet and inches                   */
#include <stdio.h>
main ()
{
/* Description  ......
   FOR each of the lengths                    [cheat261]
      Prompt for and read length in metres    [cheat262]
      Convert and output in feet and inches   [cheat263]
*/
   const int num_of_lengths = 10 ;

/* Other main program declarations            [cheat264] */


}

/* Function to convert metres to feet and inches */
void metric_imperial (flcat metres, int *feet, int *inches)
{
/* Description  ......
   Convert length in metres to inches         [cheat265]
   Compute length in inches and feet          [cheat266]
*/
   const float inches_per_metre = 39.39 ;

   int   length_in_inches ;


}
```

Figure 10.13

```
/* Reads a date, then outputs that date and the date */
/* exactly six months later, both in standard form   */
#include <stdio.h>
main ()
{
/* Description  ......
   Prompt for and get date in the form dd mm yyyy  [cheat267]
   Display date in standard form dd/mm/yy          [cheat268]
   Display date 6 months hence in form dd/mm/yy    [cheat269]
*/
   int day,
       month,
       year ;
   void display_date (int, int, int) ;


}

/* Function to display a date in the form dd/mm/yy [cheat270] */
```

Figure 10.14

```
/* Analyses text to obtain the first and last letter of each word */
#include <stdio.h>
    FILE *ex1008 ;
main ()
{
/* Description  ......
   Open file                                  [cheat271]
   Get letters from first word                [cheat272]
   WHILE not the endmarker word               [cheat273]
      Display first and last letters          [cheat274]
      Get letters from next word              [cheat275]
   Display new line                           [cheat276]
   Close the input file                       [cheat277]
*/

/* Main program declarations                  [cheat278] */


}

/* Function to obtain first and last letters of a word */
void get_letters (char *first, char *last)
{
/* Description  ......
   Read a character                           [cheat279]
   WHILE character is a space                 [cheat280]
      Read the next character                 [cheat281]
   Assign character to first letter           [cheat282]
   WHILE character not a space or full stop   [cheat283]
      Assign character to last letter         [cheat284]
      Read the next character                 [cheat285]
*/
   char character ;


}
```

Figure 10.15

11

Testing and debugging

11.1   What is testing?

Testing is the activity of trying to discover errors that may exist in a computer program. This is an important aspect of the development process; we must make every effort to ensure that our programs work correctly.

A principle to guide us is, 'Test as early as possible in the development process.' In this way any errors (bugs) will be easier to find and consequently easier (and cheaper) to correct. Obviously, errors could occur in the logic or structure of the outline design. To eliminate such errors we should employ a form of testing as we progressively develop the outline design.

For the moment we shall concentrate on trying to find errors that might exist in the code we have produced from a given outline design. We shall break this down into three stages: checking for syntax errors, manually checking for errors in the logic, and testing for logical errors by running the program.

11.2   Checking for syntax errors

Of course, the computer (compiler) checks for errors in the grammar of the programming language (syntax errors), but it is still a good idea to go over our code and to make the following checks:

1. Ensure that every identifier referred to has been declared and is of the correct type.
2. Check for consistency of usage of identifiers. For example, for a file, have we referred to it consistently in the declarations and in read (`fscanf`) or write (`fprintf`) statements?

3. Check that all necessary semicolons are present.
4. Check that all brackets, braces and parentheses match (that is, one left-hand one for each right-hand one).
5. Is our writing clear? This is particularly important if somebody else is going to type our program for us. For example, have we distinguished carefully between 0 (zero) and the letter O, between 5 and the letter S, between 1 and 7? Even if we enter the program ourselves, we may misread our own writing. Also, when examining a printout for errors, carefully check where zero and the letter O have been used, as they can often look very similar at a first glance.

11.3   Manual testing for logical errors

This involves using appropriate test data to work through the program or program fragment in question with the aid of pencil and paper.

There is a tendency for people to make the same mistake when hand testing that they made in developing the code. To overcome this, rather than attempting to elaborate the program mentally, it is a good idea to draw up a trace table and work through the code systematically. Alternatively, getting someone else to check our work can help.

11.4   Computer testing

Here we mean the execution of the program with specific test data cases designed to try to find any errors that may be in the program. This is complementary to the manual testing.

Before executing the program with a specific test case, we should always define the expected results required by the problem specification. After a test execution, we should thoroughly inspect the results achieved and compare these with our expectations.

If we find an error, we must not immediately think that this is the only one to be found in a particular execution. We should try to find others. When testing one aspect of a program we may discover something else is incorrect.

11.5   Creating test data cases

Exhaustive testing of software can often be impractical because the total number of input cases is too large to investigate. Therefore, designing good test data is of the utmost importance. Note that good test data are test data with the highest probability of detecting errors.

Consider the following checklist.

1. Identify the classes of data required and ensure that we use at least one set of data from each class. For example, a program processing integers may perform different actions for input values in the two ranges 0 to 10, 20 to 30.

2. Always include data representing the boundary cases (that is, extremes of classes, smallest and largest allowable values). When searching for a value be sure to allow for that value being first and last in the list.
3. Test cases must be written for invalid and unexpected input conditions; these are often the cases that find the errors. They are part of ensuring that the program does not do what it is supposed not to do.
4. Test the program's logic (that is, loops and conditions) as thoroughly as possible. Testing each compound relational expression with true and false is a rather weak approach. For each compound expression we should try to ensure that all combinations of the simple expressions are evaluated.
5. Having selected test data, carefully record them with the reasons for their use and their expected results; this is often referred to as the *test plan*.

11.6   Correcting errors (debugging)

We normally discover that there are errors in a program by witnessing the symptoms of the error. For example, the program appears to be in an infinite (never-ending) loop because nothing seems to be happening or the output is being repeated.

So, the process of correction must be preceded by a process of fault diagnosis. This can be the hardest part of the programming task, but it can also be the most rewarding (especially if it is someone else's fault we have diagnosed). In any sphere of diagnosis, one builds up a repertoire of symptoms and possible causes. Let us consider just a few:

1. *Symptom*   The program is giving results that are far too high.
   Possible causes   Incorrect calculation; failure to initialize a variable properly or in the wrong place.
2. *Symptom*   The program runs out of disk space.
   Possible causes   NOT generally a shortage of disk space. The program is likely to be in an infinite loop in which there is a statement that writes to disk. This may be caused by an incorrect terminating condition. If the condition is correct, it could be caused by failure to initialize a variable that controls the loop, or failure to increment a counter, or doing it in the wrong place, or forgetting a read statement.
3. *Symptom*   The program is apparently doing nothing.
   Possible causes   Again the program is probably in a loop for reasons as above. Also there may be incorrectly structured conditional statements (that is, conditions that can never be true, for example, ((number == 1) && (number > 2)).
4. *Symptom*   Not all of the data have been processed or the program runs out of data.
   Possible causes   The end of data markers might be wrong in the test case or the program might have an incorrect condition.

Having diagnosed the fault, we must then decide on the appropriate correction, check it, then implement it. When we make such a change to our program we must now make sure it has not introduced further errors as well as ensuring that it corrects the error it is designed to. So, we must retest with all previous test data cases.

11.7 Using a debugging tool

Testing the code will obviously involve using the computer, so the programmer might be able to utilize testing software such as trace programs and debugging aids. These vary considerably from computer to computer. We will consider the facilities most commonly available.

A debugger is a software tool that enables the programmer to examine various aspects of his program at the instant of execution. For instance, we may arrange to stop the program at various points in order to examine the contents of some variables. Or we might wish to see exactly the order of execution of certain components. Let us examine some of the most common features of a debugger. If you have access to such a piece of software, you might like to match its facilities with the following generalized descriptions.

1. *Variable inspection and modification*   This lets you examine the current value of variables and expressions. You can also change the value of a variable.
2. *Monitoring*   You can set up a number of monitors in a special window. Each one can be a variable or expression. As the values of these are changed during execution, their new values are shown in the window.
3. *Breakpoints*   You can mark lines in your program as breakpoints. When your program is executing and comes to a breakpoint, it will stop and show the source code with the breakpoint highlighted. You may then examine the current values of variables, or run the program up to another breakpoint. Breakpoints may be toggled on and off.
4. *Tracing*   Tracing is a means by which your program is run statement by statement. It can be used very successfully in conjunction with monitoring variable contents.

Exercises

1. Refer to Section 11.4. Why should we produce expected results before executing a program with a particular test case?
2. Refer to Section 11.5. Why is testing a relational expression for true or false a weak approach to testing?
3. Refer to Section 11.6. What problem might occur when we correct an error? How can we help to guard against this?
4. Examine the program in EX1104.C (see Fig. 11.1). It is designed to produce some simple statistical output from a list of real numbers provided in an input

file. The first line of the input file contains either LIST or NOLIST and is used
to indicate whether the input list is to be listed to the screen. The second line
contains the end-of-list marker that must be any real number greater than any
number in the list. The list then follows, terminated, of course, by the end
marker.

You are required to correct the program as follows.
(i)   Correct the syntax errors.
(ii) Produce expected results for the following data:

```
LIST
99911.9999
23.4
16.9
25.05
111.7
20.4
99911.9999
```

(iii) Run the program with the above data (in EX1104.DAT), then correct the
      logical errors.
(iv) Design test data cases to test the program as fully as possible. For each of
      your test data cases, produce expected results. Then put it all into practice
      using the computer.

5. This exercise is for those who have access to a debugger. The aim is to give
   instruction in the use of debugging tools, not merely to find the bugs in the
   program. You are encouraged to use the exercise as a means of developing a
   strategy for tackling debugging problems.

   Work through the following steps:
   (i)   Execute your copy of the program EX1105.C (given as Fig. 11.2), and
         observe the results. Using the formula for the sum of 1, 2,.., n as $n(n+1)/2$,
         answer:
         (a) Which output values are correct?
         (b) Are the incorrect values too large or too small?
         (c) From the listing determine which variables are suspect.
   (ii) Using the debugger, step through the program a statement at a time until
         you reach the first while statement.
   (iii) Inspect the contents of the variables nmax and nextval. They should be
         5 and 1 respectively.
   (iv) Put a breakpoint on the line containing the last printf statement.
   (v)   Run the program up to the breakpoint. What values should the variables
         nmax, sum and nextval have?
   (vi) Display the actual values of nmax, sum and nextval. Are the values
         correct? You will find it helpful to draw up a table, like a trace table to
         compare the expected values of these variables with their computed values,
         for the rest of the exercise. If you wish you may refer to Fig. 11.3, which

        contains this trace table.

(vii) Continue the program until it reaches the breakpoint again. Repeat this process until you have observed all of the values.

(viii) Can you see a mistake and a way of correcting the program? There are two solutions. One is to initialize sum in a different place, and the other is to initialize nextval in a different place. We will consider the second of these. The initialization of nextval should take place within the outer loop at the same point as the initialization of sum.

(ix) Verify that the program will now work provided that nextval is initialized every time the outer loop is entered.

```
/* A Very Simple Statistical Package */
#include <string.h>
main ()
{
/* Description  ......
   Display titles, read LIST/NOLIST and delimiter
   Read first number and initialize counts etc.
   WHILE not end of input list
       Process a number and read the next one
   Compute and display final results
*/
   float sum;
         average,
         smallest,
         largest ;         /* used in calculations */
   float number ;          /* current number read */
   int   count ;           /* count of numbers */
   char  listflag [7] ;    /* LIST or NOLIST */
   float delimiter ;       /* list delimiter */
   FILE  *ex1104 = fopen ("ex1104.dat", "r") ;

   printf (" Welcome to AVSSP\n\n") ;
   fscanf (ex1104, "%s", listflag) ;
   fscanf (ex1104, "%f", delimiter) ;
   count = 0 ;
   sum = 0 ;
   smallest = number ;
   largest = number ;
   fscanf (ex1104, "%f", &number);
   while (number == delimiter)
      {
      sum += number ;
      count += 1 ;
      if number > largest
         largest = number ;
      if (number > smallest)
         smallest = number ;
      if (! (strcmp (listflag, "LIST")))
         printf ("%10d %.2f\n", count, number) ;
      }
      printf ("Summary of results\n) ;
      printf ("Number of data items = %d\n", count) ;
      if (count != 0)
         {
         average = sum / count ;
         printf ("Average is : %.2f\n", average) ;
         printf ("Maximum is : %.2f\n", largest) ;
         printf ("Minimum is : %.2f\n", smallest) ;
         printf (" Range is : %.2f\n", largest - smallest) ;
}
```

Figure 11.1

```
/* This program calculates and prints the sums of */
/* the first N integers for N=5,10,15.....40      */
#include <stdio.h>
main ()
{
   const int firstsum = 5,
             lastsum  = 40,
             step     = 5 ;

   int   sum,
         nextval,
         nmax ;

   printf ("THIS PROGRAM CALCULATES THE SUM OF 1 TO N\n") ;
   printf ("N=5,10,15,....,40\n\n") ;
   nmax = firstsum ;
   nextval = 1 ;
   while (nmax <= lastsum)
      {
      sum = 0 ;
      while (nextval <= nmax)
         {
         sum += nextval ;
         ++ nextval ;
         }
      printf ("SUM OF 1,2,3,... %d = %d\n", nmax, sum) ;
      nmax += step ;
      }
}
```

Figure 11.2

Actual values			Expected values		
nmax	sum	nextval	nmax	sum	nextval
5	15	6	5	15	6
10	40	11	10	55	11
15	65	16	15	120	16
20	90	21	20	210	21
25	115	26	25	325	26
30	140	31	30	465	31
35	165	36	35	630	36
40	190	41	40	820	41

Figure 11.3

12

An introduction to program design

12.1 High-quality software

The problems that we solve in programming are usually well defined in that the
end or objective is reasonably specified, though this is not always the case. For the
purposes of this book we will assume that the problem is well understood.
However, the ways of solving the problem are various. We want to choose the best
way according to some recognized criteria.

Our goal as professionals is to provide high-quality software solutions. We want
to use a method of proceeding from problem specification to high-quality software
solution in a reasonable manner. First of all, we need to define what we mean by
high quality.

We cannot simply assume that everyone has the same understanding of the term
'high quality'. There are many factors that affect quality. For our purposes, we can
choose five basic characteristics. If these are present to an acceptable level in our
software then we can say it is of high quality. Our five indicators of quality are:

- Correctness
- Reliability
- Modifiability
- Simplicity and clarity
- Efficiency

A program is correct if it satisfies its specification completely, by performing
the tasks required of it in every respect and in as straightforward a manner as
possible. Conversely, if a program does not do what is requested of it, then it is not
correct.

The reliability of a piece of software may be stated in terms of the number of times it performs the required tasks over a number of different runs. Remember, most computer programs will operate on different sets of data each time they are run. In simple terms, a piece of software that fails to work properly, on average, once a week is less reliable than a program that fails to work, on average, once every three months.

Nearly all computer programs will require some modification (maintenance) during their lifetime. (The exception is probably only student programs; they have a lifetime of only a few days!) The user's requirements of the software change for a variety of reasons; better ways of processing are found; residual errors need correcting. The level of maintenance required is very high in many programming departments. It is common for more than 70 per cent of the cost of all programming work to be spent on maintenance tasks alone.

To be modifiable, the end-product must be easy to understand. The solutions to the most complex of problems should be clearly documented. Only bad programmers produce unnecessarily complicated programs; good programmers only ever produce straightforward solutions.

Efficiency, or how well the program performs its tasks in terms of computer resources (time and storage), is less and less of a problem each year. This is because advances in technology bring down the cost of computing power and storage each year. However, efficiency of software development seems to become more of a problem. Factors such as the size of the software to be developed or its complexity make the management of development projects harder. As customers require more and more features from software, the more difficult the programming becomes.

12.2   Design objectives

If we are to produce software of high quality according to the above criteria, then we must use a method of design that has clearly defined objectives. A good set of objectives is:

1. To define the problem clearly, paying attention to the input data provided and the results required.
2. To achieve clear and unambiguous solutions to the problem.
3. To provide a logical method of breaking down a complex problem into more manageable components or modules.
4. To provide a step-by-step method where each step is within the intellectual limitations of the average programmer.
5. To produce solutions that are easily tested.
6. To produce programs that are easily maintainable.

The purpose of this chapter is to illustrate how an outline design can be produced from a consideration of a program specification, including the way in which input data are used to produce the required output. The informal approach outlined here goes some way towards achieving the above objectives.

12.3   Design constructs

Most computer programs, and particularly those required in a business environment involve, in the broadest sense, the transformation of some input data into one or more sets of output data. This transformation will involve the following:

1. Processing items of data that are arranged in a particular order or sequence.
2. Processing like data items that are grouped together as a repetition (or iteration) of a single process to process one item.
3. Making a choice (or selection) of processing alternatives depending on the values of some data items.

If a data file is structured so that one element of it always comes before some other element and the problem requires us to recognize the difference between the two elements then the program to do this would naturally process the necessary components in the appropriate order.

For example, a stores file may be structured so that all the receipts for a commodity always come before the issues for that commodity and we are required to write total receipts followed by total issues for each commodity. The processing of a commodity would involve the simple sequence of 'Process receipts' followed by 'Process issues'.

In looking for iterations, we may look for items that are grouped together, and thus identify those components that should be processed in the same way repetitively.

For example, say a payroll file is sorted into department order (for instance, all employee records for department A followed by all records for department B and so on), and it is required to produce a list containing the total salary bill for each department. Clearly we will be processing groups of records corresponding to a department iteratively. In other words we would produce a program that has a component 'Process a department' and a control structure that executes this component repeatedly until all departments have been processed. Similarly 'Processing a department' would, in turn, involve dealing with each employee record in that department; this would be an iteration of 'Process an employee'.

In some files we may have a particular component that needs to be processed in different ways depending on some condition.

For example, a transaction file contains records of data that can be of two types. The record types appear in random order throughout the file. A program to validate the records would be likely to contain two different components that would be selected for execution depending upon the identification of the different record types.

The main program components and an outline of the program structure, in terms of sequences, iterations and selections, can be obtained from a careful analysis of the program specification and in particular the structure of the data. We also need to identify the elementary operations (such as 'Write   detail   line', 'Accumulate total' etc.) that should be associated with each component. In this respect, it is useful to ask whether the component needs any of the following:

- Input/output operations
- Initialization and finalization operations, particularly before and after an iteration
- Computation/transformation operations

Remember that as far as input operations are concerned, when processing an arbitrary length list of items (or records) we use the read-ahead technique. We read immediately after opening the file and again as soon as an item (record) has been processed.

In this book we have used a *pseudocode* representation of the program design as a program description within the source programs. We will now describe how we can arrive at such representations from a problem specification that includes sample sets of both input and output data.

Please bear in mind that each statement in the design should be in a form that could easily be translated into a small number of straightforward lines of C code. For the three programs that follow we have only coded the outline design for the third problem.

12.4   A straightforward problem

Consider the following simple problem specification. A program is required to produce a report containing a line for each record in the input file together with a heading at the start and a line containing a record count at the end. Given the following shortened sample input file (with an appropriate end marker)

```
Mike Fox      Teacher
Jim Bull      Doctor
John Turner Dentist
ZZZZZZZZZZ XXXXXXX
```

the program would produce

```
Occupations File List
   Mike Fox      Teacher
   Jim Bull      Doctor
   John Turner Dentist
Number of records in file = 3
```

We can identify from this specification that the program must have three components in sequence:

```
Write report headings
Produce the report lines
Write the record count
```

Basic program initialization would precede this sequence, and program finalization would follow it. Hence the above sequence must be preceded by an operation to prepare the files for processing, including read-ahead, and must be followed by a component to close the files. We now have:

```
Prepare to process the files and read-ahead
Write report headings
Produce the report lines
Write the record count
Close the files
```

This represents our first-level design. We must now refine it to add any necessary details. All but one of the above components may be easily translated into our programming language; 'Produce the report lines' is the one component that must be further described. Each line is produced from a single record in the input file and each record is processed in exactly the same way. Clearly, this component is a repetition or iteration of components that deal with the processing of a single record and a report line. The repetition will continue while there are records to process, that is until the end of the file. Thus, we can define this by

```
WHILE not at the end of the input file
    Write a detail line from the current record
    Increase the record count by 1
    Read the next record
```

As we are increasing a record count, we must remember to set it to zero before we start this process. In this case, we could initialize a variable at its declaration or have a specific statement before the above iteration. The latter would give us

```
Initialize the record count (= 0)
WHILE not at the end of the input file
    Write a detail line from the current record
    Increase the record count by 1
    Read the next record
```

We can now substitute the whole of the above into our first-level design, giving us the following complete design:

```
Prepare to process the files and read-ahead
Write report headings
Initialize the record count (= 0)
WHILE not at the end of the input file
    Write a detail line from the current record
    Increase the record count by 1
```

```
   Read the next record
Write the record count
Close the files
```

12.5   A data processing problem

Records in a personnel file contain name, grade (a single letter) and Y or N to indicate whether or not the member of staff holds a degree. The end marker is a record with a name of all Zs. Suppose we want to develop a program that reads this file, which is sorted by grade of staff, and displays on the screen the number of staff in each grade who possess a degree. There are headings at the start of the output and a grand total at the end. A shortened sample input file and associated output is

```
R. Brown       A     N
C. Low         A     Y
A. Young       A     N
K. Nuttall     B     N
G. Roberts     B     Y
G. Chadwick    C     Y
I. Hamilton    C     Y
M. Land        C     N
ZZZZZZZZZZZZ   Q     X

EMPLOYEES WITH A DEGREE BY GRADE

          Grade A    1
          Grade B    1
          Grade C    2

     Grand total     4
```

We observe that processing the body of the report will be concerned with processing all of the records for the first grade to produce its total, then all of the records for the second grade, then the third and so on. Clearly we have a repetition process of processing a single grade until all grades have been processed. After this we can produce the grand total. Before we start, we must display the headings and it is likely that we will have some initializing process such as 'Initialize grand total = 0' and 'Prepare to process personnel file and read-ahead'.

Therefore, our first-level design would be:

```
Prepare to process personnel file and read-ahead
Initialize grand total = 0
Display headings
```

```
WHILE not end of file
   Process a grade
Display the grand total
Close file
```

This gives us six operations and a condition. We must now examine each of these operations in turn and decide whether or not we need to refine them into even more specific design statements. We should choose this course of action when a design component cannot be obviously coded with just a few simple lines of C.

We can see that 'Process a grade' comes into this category. This is because, for any grade, more than writing a few simple lines of code is involved; for any grade we must carry out a number of tasks. So we must now break this refinement up into its component parts. When we examine the specification, we discern that we are to process employee records in groups, that is, all employees with the same grade must be processed repetitively to obtain the total for that grade. This is made easier for us because the file is sorted by grade code.

Each of these groups is processed in exactly the same way, so our refinement for 'Process a grade' could be:

```
Initialize for current grade
WHILE not end of current grade
   Process employee record
Display grade total
```

The component 'Initialize for current grade' is necessary to allow code to initialize the grade total to zero and to store the code of the current grade we are processing so that we can check when we are at the end of that grade. We can substitute the whole of this refinement into our higher-level design to give the composite design so far:

```
Prepare to process personnel file and read-ahead
Initialize grand total = 0
Display headings
WHILE not end of file
   Initialize for current grade
   WHILE not end of current grade
      Process employee record
   Display grade total
Display the grand total
Close file
```

The component 'Process employee record' now needs further examination. It is clear that each record will have a code indicating whether or not the employee has a degree, and only those with degrees require our attention. Also, after we have processed an individual record we need to replace it with the next one. The refinement for this component is then:

```
IF employee has a degree
   Increase totals
Read the next record
```

Substituting this into our previous design gives us the final design as follows:

```
Prepare to process personnel file and read-ahead
Initialize grand total = 0
Display headings
WHILE not end of file
   Initialize for current grade
   WHILE not end of current grade
      IF employee has a degree
         Increase totals
      Read the next record
   Display grade total
Display the grand total
Close file
```

12.6   A more complex problem

Consider a sales file that is sorted by ascending order of year within ascending order of sales area code. It is required to produce a report that shows the sales details from each record, with highlighting for sales over 200. Headings are required for each area and totals are to be produced at relevant control breaks, that is, at the end of each year and area. For example, a shortened version of the sales file (with an appropriate end marker) might have values such as:

```
A 1993   23.75
A 1993  125.50
A 1993  450.00
A 1994  212.66
B 1993   50.00
B 1993   25.00
B 1994  150.00
B 1994  175.00
C 1994  168.23
C 1994  400.00
C 1994   10.00
Z 9999  999.99
```

This would produce the following output:

```
Area A sales
     A     1993      23.75
     A     1993     125.50
```

```
        A    1993      450.00    * * * * * *
Total for 1993      599.25
        A    1994      212.66    * * * * * *
Total for 1994      212.66
Total for area A    811.91

Area B sales
        B    1993       50.00
        B    1993       25.00
Total for 1993       75.00
        B    1994      150.00
        B    1994      175.00
Total for 1994      325.00
Total for area B    400.00

Area C sales
        C    1994      168.23
        C    1994      400.00    * * * * * *
        C    1994       10.00
Total for 1994      578.23
Total for area C    578.23
```

We note from the specification, particularly the output, that processing the sales report will involve, at the top level, an iteration that processes an area at a time, because although the details are different for each area the structure is the same, hence each area is processed in the same way. So we would have as our first-level design:

```
Prepare to process the files and read-ahead
WHILE not at the end of the sales file
    Process an area
Close the files
```

The next stage is to concentrate on the processing required for an area. An area in the output consists of a heading, then the details for that area, then the area total. We must, therefore, incorporate a sequence of 'Write   area   heading', 'Process   area   details' and then 'Write   area   total'. Also, we recognize the need for an initialization operation, 'Initialize area total = 0', before processing an area's details. We substitute this sequence for 'Process an area', giving us:

```
Prepare to process the files and read-ahead
WHILE not at the end of the sales file
    Write area heading
    Initialize area total = 0
    Process area details
```

```
Write area total
Close the files
```

What processing is required for 'Process area details'? Again, an examination of the specification above reveals that the details for an area are split into
the data for different years. Also, we observe that the output for each year consists
of the detailed records for that year followed by the year total. Although there are
at most two years per area in our example, there could obviously be more, so we
will process the details for a year repetitively.

How do we recognize the terminating condition for this iteration, namely the
end of the current area? Consider again the sample file given as part of the specification.

The current area will terminate when the area code changes. If we compare the
area code of the record currently being processed with that of the previous record,
then we will know if we have started looking at a new area. Therefore, we must
store the current area code when we start processing an area. We can then continue
processing an area as long as the current area code is equal to the stored area code.

Taking all of this into account, we can revise our design as follows:

```
Prepare to process the files and read-ahead
WHILE not at the end of the sales file
    Write area heading
    Initialize area total = 0
    Store current area code
    WHILE not at the end of an area
        Process a year's details
    Write area total
Close the files
```

Again, by examining the specification including the sample data we see that processing a year involves a sequence of processing the body of the year (that is all of
the main details) and then writing the year total. Noting that the body of the year is
an iteration, that we need to initialize a total for each year and recognize the end of
a particular year, we arrive at the following as the details for 'Process a
year's details':

```
Initialize year total = 0
Store current year
WHILE not at the end of a year
    Process a detail line
Write year total
```

We can substitute this into our design as follows:

```
Prepare to process the files and read-ahead
WHILE not at the end of the sales file
    Write area heading
```

```
   Initialize area total = 0
   Store current area code
   WHILE not at the end of an area
      Initialize year total = 0
      Store current year
      WHILE not at the end of a year
         Process a detail line
      Write year total
   Write area total
Close the files
```

Processing an individual record (detail line) involves writing the details to the output file, adding the highlighting if required, accumulating the totals and then reading the next record as follows:

```
Write details to output
IF high sales value
   Write asterisks
Add sales value to year total
Add sales value to area total
Read the next record
```

The complete design is now obtained by substituting this refinement for 'Process a detail line' into our previous higher-level design to give the following:

```
Prepare to process the files and read-ahead
WHILE not at the end of the sales file
   Write area heading
   Initialize area total = 0
   Store current area code
   WHILE not at the end of an area
      Initialize year total = 0
      Store current year
      WHILE not at the end of a year
         Write details to output
         IF high sales value
            Write asterisks
         Add sales value to year total
         Add sales value to area total
         Read the next record
      Write year total
   Write area total
Close the files
```

The complete C program is given as Fig. 12.1.

```
/* Program to print sales anaylsis */
#include <stdio.h>
main ()
{
/* Description  ......
   Prepare to process the files and read-ahead
   WHILE not at the end of the sales file
       Write area heading
       Initialize area total = 0
       Store current area code
       WHILE not at the end of an area
           Initialize year total = 0
           Store current year
           WHILE not at the end of a year
               Write details to output
               IF high sales value
                   Write asterisks
               Add sales value to year total
               Add sales value to area total
               Read the next record
           Write year total
       Write area total
   Close the files
*/
    char    area,
            stored_area ;
    int     year,
            stored_year ;
    float   sales_value,
            area_total,
            year_total ;
    FILE  *input_file = fopen ("sales.dat", "r") ;
    FILE  *output_file = fopen ("report.dat", "w") ;

    fscanf (input_file, "%c%d%f\n", &area, &year, &sales_value) ;
    while (area != 'Z')
        {
        fprintf (output_file, "Area %c sales\n", area) ;
        area_total = 0 ;
        stored_area = area ;
        while (area == stored_area)
            {
            year_total = 0 ;
            stored_year = year ;
            while ((area == stored_area) && (year == stored_year))
                {
                fprintf (output_file, "     %c%8d%10.2f" , area, year,
                    sales_value) ;
                if (sales_value > 200)
                    fprintf (output_file, "    ******") ;
```

Figure 12.1

```
                 fprintf (output_file, "\n") ;
                 year_total += sales_value ;
                 area_total += sales_value ;
                 fscanf (input_file, "%c%d%f\n", &area, &year,
                    &sales_value) ;
                 }
             fprintf (output_file, "Total for %4d%10.2f\n",
                stored_year, year_total) ;
             }
          fprintf (output_file, "Total for area %c%8.2f\n\n",
             stored_area, area_total) ;
          }
      fclose (input_file) ;
      fclose (output_file) ;
}
```

Figure 12.1 Continued.

Exercises

For each of the following specifications, design a program using the step-by-step approach outlined in this chapter.

1. A production file contains a number of records about machines, indicating whether or not they are due for replacement. It is required to produce a duplicate file, without the end marker but with an extra record at the end containing a count of the machines that are due for replacement. For example, an abbreviated input file of

```
Lathe Yes
Drill No
Saw   Yes
ZZZZZ XX
```

would give an output file of

```
Lathe Yes
Drill No
Saw   Yes
2 machines due for replacement
```

2. A hospital file contains records of staff and patients sorted into ascending order of surname within ascending order of ward. It is required to write the names of all the staff in ward order, with a heading at the start of each ward. For example, an abbreviated input file of

```
Ward A Bill Jones    Patient
```

```
Ward A Jean Ogden    Staff
Ward B Paul Brown    Staff
Ward B Vera Burns    Patient
Ward B John Smith    Staff
Ward Z XXXXXXXXXXXX XXXXXXX
```

would give the following output:

```
Ward A headings
   Jean Ogden
Ward B headings
   Paul Brown
   John Smith
```

3. A product file contains a number of product records. Each record contains an area code (a single letter), a district code (three digits), a product code (a single letter) and a value (integer). The file is sorted into ascending order of district code within ascending order of area. A program is required to select records with a product code of the letter C and produce a report showing district and area totals of the values of the selected records in the order implied by the product file. For example, the abbreviated input file

```
A 001 C 300
A 001 G 150
A 002 B 200
A 002 C 500
B 002 C 120
B 002 C 320
B 003 G 100
Z 999 X 999
```

would give the following report:

```
Area A District 001 total 300
Area A District 002 total 500
            Area A total 800
Area B District 002 total 440
Area B District 003 total   0
            Area B total 440
```

4. A student application file contains records which hold the status of applicants. The file is sorted into ascending order of course code. For each course there may be records of applicants who have been offered a place followed by records of applicants who have been rejected.

It is required to produce a listing containing a report for each course of all rejected applicants. The reports contain a heading followed by the various applicants' names (one per line) followed by a total of such names. For example, the abbreviated application file

```
A10  Katie Green      Offered
A10  William Smith    Rejected
A10  Jack Howard      Rejected
G12  Olive Brown      Offered
G12  Audrey Stevens Offered
G12  Jim Taylor       Rejected
Z99  XXXXXXXXXXXXXX XXXXXXXX
```

would give the following listing:

```
    Course A10 - Report
William Smith
Jack Howard
Total students rejected 2
    Course G12 - Report
Jim Taylor
Total students rejected 1
```

13

Introduction to arrays

13.1 The need for arrays

So far we have dealt with individual data values that could be stored in a single variable. In reality, we often have to deal with an ordered collection of similar, related items. Consider some examples.

1. A vector could be regarded as an ordered collection of real numbers.
2. A line of text could be regarded as an ordered collection of characters.
3. Prices of all the goods in a shop could be regarded as an ordered collection of integers (that is, price in pence).

If the problem requires us to store such related values for later use in the program, then it is neither convenient nor sensible to declare a large number of individual variables.

Let us consider an example. A firm employs a group of four salesmen, with reference numbers 1 to 4, who are awarded a bonus if their sales exceed two-thirds of the average sales for the group. A program is required to read in the sales of each of the salesmen and display the reference number and sales of those who qualify for the bonus. We could declare four variables, say `sales1`, `sales2`, `sales3`, `sales4` and use the code as shown in Fig. 13.1.

Imagine how cumbersome this would be if we had twenty salesmen! Ideally, we would like to use some form of repetition or looping, but we are unable to do so with our present knowledge of C. The problem can be overcome by using *arrays*.

```
fscanf (inpfile, "%d%d%d%d", &sales1, &sales2, &sales3, &sales4) ;
bonus_level = 2.0 / 3.0 * (sales1 + sales2 + sales3 + sales4) / 4 ;
if (sales1 > bonus_level)
    printf ("Salesman 1 %d\n", sales1) ;
if (sales2 > bonus_level)
    printf ("Salesman 2 %d\n", sales2) ;
if (sales3 > bonus_level)
    printf ("Salesman 3 %d\n", sales3) ;
if (sales4 > bonus_level)
    printf ("Salesman 4 %d\n", sales4) ;
```

Figure 13.1

13.2   Arrays in C

So that a suitable amount of storage can be reserved, we must declare arrays by stating the following:

- The type of the values to be stored.
- A variable identifier by which we can refer to the array.
- The number of elements in the array.

Consider the following array declarations:

```
float sales [4] ;                                    (13-1)

int   price [100] ;                                  (13-2)
```

In (13-1) we have an array of 4 floating point elements, and in (13-2) we have an array of 100 integer elements.

In the array sales [4], declared above, we have a size of four elements. We can now picture an array called sales with four store locations each capable of holding a real value. Each store location is identified by means of an *index* sometimes known as a *subscript*. According to C conventions, the index will have a lower bound of zero and, in this case, an upper bound of three. This is illustrated in Fig. 13.2.

The first store location is for the element of sales with an index of zero, the second store location is for the element of sales with an index of one, the third store location is for the element of sales with an index of two and the fourth store location is for the element of sales with an index of three.

We can access any particular element of the array, use its value in an expression, and assign it a new value in exactly the same way as we have been doing with a simple variable. We distinguish the elements by using the appropriate index value between square brackets. The index can be expressed directly as an integer constant, or the value of an integer variable, or the value of an integer expression. For example,

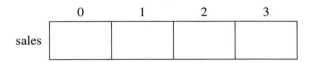

Figure 13.2

```
        0        1        2        3
sales │ 30.1  │ 12.5  │        │ 42.6  │
```

Figure 13.3

```
index = 3 ;
sales [1] = 12.5 ;
sales [0] = 30.1 ;
sales [index] = sales [index - 2] + sales [0] ;
```

would give the results shown in Fig. 13.3.

The value of the index must be between zero and one less than the declared size of the array. For example, building on the above,

```
sales [4] = 20.5 ;
sales [index + 2] = 10 ;
```

would both give an error.

The power of the index notation lies in the fact that we can use any suitable expression as the index. For example, we can set all one hundred elements of price to zero by means of

```
for (counter = 0 ; counter < 100 ; ++ counter)
   price [counter] = 0 ;
```

Let us consider a complete program that uses an array. The sales figures of twenty salesmen, having reference numbers of 1 to 20, are held in a sales file in reference number order. Figure 13.4 is the program that displays salesmen who qualify for a bonus because their sales exceed two-thirds of the average.

Note the use of the statement in the fourth line:

```
#define SALESMEN 20
```

This is a symbolic constant associating the value 20 with the identifier SALESMEN whenever it is used in a program. It is a common convention to use uppercase letters when defining symbolic constants, and it is considered good programming practice to use them to define the index size of arrays. If the program had to be altered to allow for a different number of salesmen, then only the constant definition would need to be changed. There is a discussion of #define in Chapter 18.

```
/* Reads the sales of 20 salesmen, outputs the salesman's */
/* reference and sales of those who qualify for bonus.    */
#include <stdio.h>
#define SALESMEN 20
main ()
{
/* Description  ......
   Open input file
   Initialize total (= 0)
   FOR each salesman in turn
      Read sales figure into array, accumulate total
   Compute bonus level
   FOR each salesman in turn
      Output when sales figure > bonus level
   Close input file
*/
   float sales [SALESMEN] ;
   int   index ;
   float total_sales,
         bonus_level ;
   FILE *salesfile = fopen ("salesfil.dat", "r") ;

   total_sales = 0 ;
   for (index = 0 ; index < SALESMEN ; ++ index)
      {
      fscanf (salesfile, "%f", &sales [index]) ;
      total_sales += sales [index] ;
      }
   bonus_level = 2.0 / 3.0 * (total_sales / SALESMEN) ;
   for (index = 0 ; index < SALESMEN ; ++ index)
      if (sales [index] > bonus_level)
         printf ("Salesman %2d %.2f\n", index + 1, sales [index]) ;
   fclose (salesfile) ;
}
```

Figure 13.4

The program is essentially two loops, both of which access each element of the array `sales` in turn using the `for` statement. Hence, the `for` statement control is the same:

```
for (index = 0 ; index < SALESMEN ; ++ index)
```

The first loop demonstrates a standard technique for reading elements into an array and at the same time producing a total value from its elements. The initialization, `total_sales = 0`, before entering the loop is necessary because inside the loop there is a statement to add to the existing value in `total_sales`. The `printf` statement in the second loop will display the salesman's reference number followed by his sales. The reference number is one greater than the index

	0	1	2	3	4	5	6	7	8	9
table	25	13	7	0	5	17	98	22	31	40

Figure 13.5

because locations 0 to 19 are used to hold the sales for salesmen with reference numbers 1 to 20.

13.3   Table look-up

In certain programs, we may wish to examine a list (or table) of values to see if it includes a particular value. We look through the list to determine whether or not the required value occurs anywhere in the list.

For example, if `table` is declared as an array of integer values we could visualize it by means of Fig. 13.5.

With a required value or target of 17 we should find that `table` `[5]` matches this target. With a target of 50 we should find that no component of `table` matches the target.

A simple algorithm to effect this kind of table searching would be to use a variable, such as `found`, that we first initialize to -1, an impossible index value. Then we go through the table one element at a time from the beginning, changing `found` to the current index value and terminating the search if we find the target value in the table. On completing this process, we could display an appropriate message depending on the value of `found`.

A typical program incorporating such a linear search, or *table look-up*, is given in Fig. 13.6.

In this program we see one way of initializing an array.

```
int table [TABLE_LENGTH] = {25, 13, 7, 0, 5, 17, 98,
                            22, 31, 40} ;
```

This statement declares the array `table` and initializes it such that `table` `[0]` is 25, `table` `[1]` is 13, and so on. If the list of initial values in braces is shorter than the number of array elements to be initialized, the remaining elements are initialized to zero. This allows a shorthand way of initializing all elements of an array to zero:

```
int table [10] = {0} ;
```

If an array is declared without a size and is given initial values, the size is implied from the number of values in the list. For example,

```
int table [] = {23, 34, 54, 32} ;
```

declares an array of size four with the initial values as in the list.

```
/* Program to demonstrate a table look-up */
#include <stdio.h>
#define TABLE_LENGTH 10
main ()
{
/* Description  ......
    Prompt for and read target value
    Initialize found (= -1)
    FOR each location in the table or until target found
        IF value in table = target
            Store location in found
    IF target found
        Display location in table
    ELSE
        Display not found message
*/
    int location,
        found,
        target ;
    int table [TABLE_LENGTH] = {25, 13, 7, 0, 5, 17, 98,
                                22, 31, 40} ;

    printf ("Enter target value ") ;
    scanf ("%d", &target) ;
    found = -1 ;
    for (location = 0 ; (location < TABLE_LENGTH)
        && (found == -1) ; ++ location)
        if (table [location] == target)
            found = location ;
    if (found != -1)
        printf ("Target found at location %d\n", found) ;
    else
        printf ("Target not found\n") ;
}
```

Figure 13.6

13.4   Strings as arrays

In Chapter 8 we saw that string variables could be declared as arrays of type
char. For example, char name [12] is a string variable, name, defined as an
array of eleven char elements plus the end marker (\0).

For character arrays, we have two ways of specifying initial values:

char vowels [] = {'A', 'E', 'I', 'O', 'U'} ;   (13-3)

char vowels [] = "AEIOU" ;   (13-4)

In both cases, the character array (string) vowels has a size of six with contents
of AEIOU terminated by the invisible end marker (\0) for a string. Clearly,

Example (13-4) is a very convenient shorthand and is the form we have been using for string values.

We have also seen in Chapter 8 that it is possible to use scanf (and fscanf) to read strings, but this has certain limitations. When we use scanf all characters up to the first space, tab or newline character are read into the array. This means that if we want to have any spaces within our string, we must use some other method to read them. Also, we noted that it is the programmer's responsibility to ensure that the string variable is not over-filled, that is, a program should never attempt to put more characters in the string than the size defined in its declaration.

The C language provides specific functions to read and write strings. For example, the function fgets reads a string of a specified maximum size from a file. This helps to overcome the limitations we have identified when using fscanf. We shall look at fgets in Chapter 17.

Exercises

1. How would you amend the example program in Fig. 13.4 to match the following specification changes?
   (i) Display an appropriate screen heading and column headings.
   (ii) Display the reference number of the best salesman below the table.
   (iii) The input data are in no specific order but each line of the sales file now contains the salesman's reference number and then the sales figure.
2. Refer to the table look-up example in Fig. 13.6. If the table was sorted into ascending order of values, how could we improve the efficiency of this algorithm?
3. Declare and give initial values to two arrays. The first is to contain all prime numbers up to 23, the second to contain all letters that can be used as roman numerals.
4. An input file (EX1304.DAT) consists of eight real numbers. Design and code a program to calculate the average of these numbers and determine which values, together with their positions in the input file, are greater than the average. For example, if the input file contains

```
4.1 10.5 8.0 4.2 7.1 3.5 9.0 3.2
```

then the following output should be displayed on the screen:

```
Average is 6.2
Values > average    Position
      10.5              2
       8.0              3
       7.1              5
       9.0              7
```

Design and code the program. Should you need help, EX1304.C is available as an outline design on the course disk, together with appropriate cheats.

```
/* Uses a bubble sort on contents of a file */
#include <stdio.h>
#define TOTAL_ITEMS 100
main ()
{
/* Description  ......
   Read input file into array                     [cheat328]
   FOR pass is 1 to TOTAL_ITEMS - 1               [cheat329]
      FOR index is 0 to TOTAL_ITEMS - pass - 1    [cheat330]
         IF current item > next one               [cheat331]
            Swap items round                      [cheat332]
   FOR index is 0 to TOTAL_ITEMS - 1              [cheat333]
      Output current item                         [cheat334]
   Close the input file                           [cheat335]
*/
   int    items [TOTAL_ITEMS] ;
   int    index,
          pass,
          temp ;
   FILE *ex1307 = fopen ("ex1307.dat", "r") ;

}
```

Figure 13.7

5. A file (EX1305.DAT) contains the marks gained by a class of students in an examination. It is required to adjust the marks such that, if the highest mark is less than 75, all marks are increased by 10 and displayed on the screen. A maximum of twenty marks is in the file and it is terminated by a mark of 999.

   Design and code the program to adjust the marks. Should you need help, EX1305.C is available as an outline design on the course disk, together with appropriate cheats.

6. An input file (EX1306.DAT) consists of a table of the ten integer codes for courses run by a college, with one course code per line. Another input file (EX1306A.DAT) contains a sequence of course codes, taken from application forms, one code per line with a code of 9999 as an end marker. It is required to validate each of the course codes in EX1306A.DAT by comparing them with the codes in the table and then displaying the course code with an appropriate message on the screen.

   Design and code the program. Should you need help, EX1306.C is available as an outline design on the course disk, together with appropriate cheats.

7. The design given in EX1307.C (see Fig. 13.7) is for a program that reads the file EX1307.DAT containing one hundred numbers into an array, then sorts the array into ascending order, then displays the array on the screen. You are required to code and test this program.

14

Multi-dimensional arrays

14.1 Examples of multi-dimensional arrays

In the previous chapter, we met *one-dimensional* arrays, that is, arrays whose components are single data items (single numbers, characters and so on). An array whose elements are themselves one-dimensional arrays is called a *two-dimensional* array. Likewise, we can define three-dimensional arrays and so on.

Consider a table of exam marks obtained by a class of eight students in each of four papers. This is illustrated in Fig. 14.1.

student	paper index			
index	0	1	2	3
0	33	51	27	20
1	83	90	20	85
2	99	35	65	10
::	::	::	::	::
7	50	71	48	53

Figure 14.1

The marks of one student could be stored in a one-dimensional array as follows:

```
#define PAPERS 4
int marks [PAPERS] ;
```

The complete marks table could also be stored in a one-dimensional array:

```
#define MARKS 32
int marks [MARKS] ;
```

But this is not very convenient if we want to access all of a single student's marks or all of the marks for one paper. What indexes would we use? Does the index range 0 to 3 mean the four marks for the first student or the first four marks for the first paper? A two-dimensional array solves the problem:

```
#define STUDENTS 8
#define PAPERS 4
int marks [STUDENTS] [PAPERS] ;
```

Now we can apply two indexes to our array of marks. The first identifies the student, the second the paper. So,

```
my_mark = marks [5] [2] ;
```

would assign to my_mark the value of the marks array element whose first index is 5 (that is, the student index of 5) and second index is 2 (that is, a paper index of 2). We can think of a two-dimensional array as having rows and columns. The array marks has one row for each student and one column for each paper. Thus, marks [1]   [3] refers to the mark from row 2 (student index 1) and column 4 (paper index 3) that has the value 85 in our example in Fig. 14.1. Similarly, it can be seen that marks   [0]   [2] contains the value 27 and marks [2]   [3] has the value 10.

Since array indexes in C start at 0, marks   [0]   [2] is actually the mark obtained by the first student in the third paper and marks   [2]   [3] refers to the mark scored by the third student in the fourth paper.

Let us now consider a problem that uses the above two-dimensional array to store and access marks. Each line of an input file contains a student number in the range 0 to 7, a paper number in the range 0 to 3, and the corresponding mark. The marks have been recorded in no specific order, and, since marks of 0 are not recorded, not all marks are present in the input file. The end marker is a line with a student number of 9 and a paper number of 9.

The program given in Fig. 14.2 displays the marks on the screen in the form of a table with one row for each student and the student's total mark at the end of each row.

This example illustrates a typical situation; data are stored in the array and then the two-dimensional array is processed by two nested loops using two indexing variables. Note the position of the various initialization statements and also the printf statements.

Notice also two points of detail in respect of this particular problem. Not all the marks were recorded in the input file, so we had to ensure that any missing marks were stored as 0 by initializing all elements of the array to 0 at the start of the program.

Also, because of the values in the end marker, we had to use one fscanf statement for the student number and paper number and a separate one for the mark. Even if the end marker line had contained a value for the mark,

```
/* Program to read in marks file then output marks as a */
/* table and the total mark for each student           */
#include <stdio.h>
#define STUDENTS 8
#define PAPERS 4
main ()
{
/* Description  ......
   Initialize array - all elements zero
   Open the input file
   Read first student number and paper number
   WHILE not at end of file
      Read mark into array
      Read next student number and paper number
   Close the input file
   FOR each student in turn
      Initialize student total
      FOR each paper in turn
         Display mark
         Accumulate student total
      Display student total
*/

   int   marks [STUDENTS] [PAPERS] = { 0 } ;
   int   student_index,
         paper_index,
         student_total,
         student_number,
         paper_number ;
   FILE *marks_file = fopen ("markfile.dat", "r") ;

   fscanf (marks_file, "%d%d", &student_number, &paper_number) ;
   while (student_number != 9)
      {
      fscanf (marks_file, "%d", &marks [student_number]
         [paper_number]) ;
      fscanf (marks_file, "%d%d", &student_number,
         &paper_number) ;
      }
   fclose (marks_file) ;
   for (student_index = 0 ; student_index < STUDENTS ;
      ++ student_index)
      {
      student_total = 0 ;
      for (paper_index = 0 ; paper_index < PAPERS ;
         ++ paper_index)
         {
         printf ("%3d", marks [student_index] [paper_index]) ;
         student_total = student_total + marks [student_index]
            [paper_index] ;
         }
      printf ("%4d\n", student_total) ;
      }
}
```

Figure 14.2

row	column			
	0	1	2	3
0	5	6	1	2
1	10	16	15	19
2	41	52	73	81

Figure 14.3

```
fscanf (marks_file, "%d%d%d", &student_number,
    &paper_number, &marks [student_number] [paper_number]) ;
```

would produce a run-time error when reading the end marker. Both of the array indexes would have a value of 9, which is outside their respective ranges.

Let us now consider another example. In Fig. 14.3, we show some data in the form of a three-by-four table, that is three rows and four columns, with appropriate indexes indicated.

Such an array of numbers is often referred to as a *matrix*. It could be stored in the following array:

```
#define ROWS 3
#define COLUMNS 4
int matrix [ROWS] [COLUMNS] ;
```

If the input data are typed in row order, that is

5 6 1 2 10 16 15 19 41 52 73 81

then the values could be read into the array by means of

```
for (row = 0 ; row < ROWS ; ++ row)
    for (column = 0 ; column < COLUMNS ; ++ column)
        scanf ("%d", &matrix [row] [column]) ;
```

If it is required to output the array in the form given in Fig. 14.3, we would use

```
for (row = 0 ; row < ROWS ; ++ row)
    {
    for (column = 0 ; column < COLUMNS ; ++ column)
        printf ("%5d", matrix [row] [column]) ;
    printf ("\n") ;
    }
```

Notice that the outer loop contains a `printf` statement to write a new line at the end of each row.

Outputting the matrix in transposed form (that is, rows become columns) would give:

```
5     10    41
6     16    52
1     15    73
2     19    81
```

The code to achieve this is very similar to that above. Try to spot the difference.

```
for (column = 0 ; column < COLUMNS ; ++ column)
   {
   for (row = 0 ; row < ROWS ; ++ row)
      printf ("%5d", matrix [row] [column]) ;
   printf ("\n") ;
   }
```

We note that the order in which we access the matrix (row by row as in the first example, or column by column for the transformed matrix in the second example) is given by the order of nesting of the for loops, not by changing the indexes around.

The complete program to read in the three-by-four matrix and output it in its two forms is given as Fig. 14.4.

14.2   Step-by-step guide to using arrays

14.2.1 THE NEED FOR TWO-DIMENSIONAL ARRAYS

We use two-dimensional arrays when the problem requires us to store a two-dimensional table of values for later use in the program.

In the first example (shown in Fig. 14.2), if we had merely been required to display the total of all the marks recorded in the input file, then there would have been no need to store the individual marks and no need for an array. We would have read each mark and added it to the total within a single loop.

If the specification had required us to output the total mark for each student, without displaying the table of marks, then again there is no need to store all of the marks, but we would need to hold the total for each student in a one-dimensional array:

```
int student_total [STUDENTS] ;
```

As each mark and student number is read from the input file, the mark would be added to the appropriate total using a statement of the following form:

```
student_total [student_number] += mark ;
```

A second loop would then be used to display each total from the array.

```
/* Program to read 12 integers into a 3 by 4 matrix, */
/* output it as three rows by four columns and in    */
/* its transformed form                              */
#include <stdio.h>
#define ROWS 3
#define COLUMNS 4
main ()
{
/* Description  ......
   Read 12 integers into matrix and output as 3 rows
      by 4 columns
   Output matrix as 4 rows by 3 columns
*/
   int    matrix [ROWS] [COLUMNS] ;
   int    row,
          column ;

   for (row = 0 ; row < ROWS ; ++ row)
      {
      for (column = 0 ; column < COLUMNS ; ++ column)
         {
         scanf ("%d", &matrix [row] [column]) ;
         printf ("%5d", matrix [row] [column]) ;
         }
      printf ("\n") ;
      }
   for (column = 0 ; column < COLUMNS ; ++ column)
      {
      for (row = 0 ; row < ROWS ; ++ row)
         printf ("%5d", matrix [row] [column]) ;
      printf ("\n") ;
      }
}
```

Figure 14.4

14.2.2 THE FORM OF THE ARRAY AND DECLARATIONS

Having identified the need to store data in a two-dimensional array, we then have to decide how to organize the array in terms of rows and columns. For convenience, this may be determined by the order of the input data or the form of output required. But remember that once the array has been set up in one form, its elements can be accessed in any order.

Before writing the appropriate declarations, you might find it useful to draw a table with sample values. We then establish symbolic constants for both dimensions. For example,

```
#define ROWS 5
#define COLUMNS 8
```

Then declare the array variable using these constants:

```
int table [ROWS] [COLUMNS] ;
```

Then declare array index variables:

```
int row_index,
    col_index ;
```

14.2.3 READING DATA INTO THE ARRAY

The method used to read data into a two-dimensional array will depend on the way in which the data have been recorded in the input file and the structure of the array. This can be illustrated as follows:

1. The values are recorded in row order

In this case the pseudo-code would be

```
Read values row by row into array
```

or, in more detail,

```
FOR each row in turn
    FOR each column in turn
        Read a number into the array
```

with code such as

```
for (row_index = 0 ; row_index < ROWS ; ++ row_index)
    for (col_index = 0 ; col_index < COLUMNS ;
        ++ col_index)
        fscanf (inp_file, "%d", &table [row_index]
            [col_index]) ;
```

2. The values are recorded in column order

The corresponding pseudo-code would be:

```
Read values column by column into array
```

or,

```
FOR each column in turn
    FOR each row in turn
        Read a number into the array
```

with code such as

```
for (col_index = 0 ; col_index < COLUMNS ; ++ col_index)
    for (row_index = 0 ; row_index < ROWS ; ++ row_index)
        fscanf (inp_file, "%d", &table [row_index]
            [col_index]) ;
```

3. Each of the values (40 in our case) is recorded, preceded by its row and column index, but in random order

In this case, the pseudo-code would be

```
Read 40 values into array
```

or, in more detail,

```
FOR each number in turn (i.e. 40 times)
    Read row index, column index, then number into array
```

This would require an additional variable `number_count` and the corresponding C code would be

```
for (number_count = 1 ; number_count <= 40 ;
    ++ number_count)
    fscanf (inp_file, "%d%d%d", &row_index, &col_index,
        &table [row_index] [col_index]) ;
```

4. The values are recorded as in (3), except that not all of the 40 values are recorded and consequently the file will need an end marker

The pseudocode for this case would be

```
Initialize array -  all elements zero
Read file contents appropriately into array
```

or, in more detail,

```
Initialize array — all elements zero
Read first row index and column index
WHILE not at end of file
    Read a number into the array
    Read next row index and column index
```

This technique was used in the student marks example above (see Fig. 14.2).

14.2.4 DISPLAYING THE ARRAY WITH ROW AND COLUMN TOTALS

We now demonstrate how data stored in an array can be displayed on the screen together with a total at the end of each row and at the bottom of each column. Given that we have the declarations as in Section 14.2.2, we will need to store all the column totals so we also declare a one-dimensional array for the column totals (using the symbolic constant) and initialize it to zeros. Also, we declare a single variable for the row total.

```
int col_total [COLUMNS] = { 0 } ;
int row_total ;
```

The detailed pseudocode for this is

```
FOR each row in turn
    Initialize the row total to zero
    FOR each column in turn
        Display the array element
        Add array element to the row total
        Add array element to the column total
    Display the row total
FOR each column in turn
    Display the column total
Print a new line
```

The corresponding C code is

```
for (row_index = 0 ; row_index < ROWS ; ++ row_index)
    {
    row_total = 0 ;
    for (col_index = 0 ; col_index < COLUMNS ;
        ++ col_index)
        {
        printf ("%5d", table [row_index] [col_index]) ;
        row_total += table [row_index] [col_index] ;
        col_total [col_index] += table [row_index]
            [col_index] ;
        }
    printf ("%5d\n", row_total) ;
    }
for (col_index = 0 ; col_index < COLUMNS ; ++ col_index)
    printf ("%5d", col_total [col_index]) ;
printf ("\n") ;
```

Exercises

1. Refer to the program in Fig. 14.2, then answer the following:
    (i) Find the code that puts zeros into each element of the array.
    (ii) Prove that the program works by doing a dry run. Use headings for each of the elementary variables and a table for the array marks (see Fig. 14.1).
2. Using the design in EX1402.C (see Fig. 14.5), complete the program that inputs

and outputs a table of exam marks. The marks are supplied paper by paper in the input file, that is, all the marks for paper 1, followed by all the marks for paper 2 and so on. The table is to be displayed on the screen with no headings or titles with one row for each student and one column for each paper. On the right of each row, write the student's total mark. At the foot of each column, write the average mark for that paper, ignoring any decimal point (that is, using integer division). Use the input file EX1402.DAT which assumes four papers for a class of five students.

Notice that the array marks has been defined in such a way that its rows (STUDENTS) and columns (PAPERS) correspond to the rows and columns of the required output. The data in the input file are in effect in column order.

3. Using the outline design in EX1403.C (see Fig. 14.6), complete the program that reads a file of grid references and letters and plots (that is, stores) the letters at the appropriate grid reference in a matrix. The matrix has 10 rows and 12 columns. When the end of file is detected (row = 99 and column = 99), the grid is displayed at the terminal. For example, the file supplied (EX1403.DAT) contains

```
0  0A
1  2B
3  3C
4  1C
5  2D
5  3D
6  1E
7  0E
5  4D
9  11C
9  9C
99 99Z
```

This would give the following output:

```
row   0 A
row   1    B
row   2
row   3      C
row   4  C
row   5    DDD
row   6  E
row   7 E
row   8
row   9              C C
```

4. A wholesaler buys dog food from five different suppliers (we shall refer to them as suppliers 0 to 4) and in three sizes (0, 1 and 2). The amounts of money (in

pence) that the wholesaler has paid over a period of a year are stored in a file that contains in each line the supplier number, then the size, then the amount paid.

Design and write a program to calculate and display the supplier who has been paid the highest total amount for each of the sizes in turn. For example, the file (EX1404.DAT) contains the following data:

```
0 1 32
2 0 66
4 0 67
4 1 28
2 1 35
0 2 22
1 0 70
0 0 54
3 1 40
3 2 20
1 1 30
1 2 21
2 2 22
3 0 63
4 2 25
1 0 70
3 1 40
4 2 25
9 9
```

This would generate the output

```
Supplier 1 received most for size 0 tins (140 pence)
Supplier 3 received most for size 1 tins (80 pence)
Supplier 4 received most for size 2 tins (50 pence)
```

In this exercise you will need to use a two-dimensional array for the total amounts, and as you read the input data add the individual amounts to the appropriate element in the array. This implies, of course, that you will have initialized all array elements to zero.

If required, the outline design may be found in EX1404.C on the supplied disk, together with appropriate cheats.

```
/* Program to read in marks file then output */
/* table of marks                            */
#include <stdio.h>
#define STUDENTS 5
#define PAPERS 4
main ()
{
/* Description  ......
   Read file contents appropriately into array   [cheat350]
   FOR each student in turn                       [cheat351]
      Initialize student total                    [cheat352]
      FOR each paper in turn                       [cheat353]
         Output student mark                      [cheat354]
         Accumulate student total                 [cheat355]
         Accumulate paper total                   [cheat356]
      Output student total                        [cheat357]
   Calculate and output paper averages            [cheat358]
   Close the input file                           [cheat359]
*/
   int    marks [STUDENTS] [PAPERS] ;
   int    paper_index,
          student_index ;
   int    paper_total [PAPERS] = { 0 } ;
   int    student_total,
          average ;
   FILE *ex1402 = fopen ("ex1402.dat", "r") ;


}
```

Figure 14.5

```
/* Plots letters in an array then displays it as a grid */
#include <stdio.h>
#define COLUMNS 12
#define ROWS 10
main ()
{
/* Description  ......
   Prepare to read file                    [cheat361]
   Initialize array to spaces              [cheat362]
   Read file appropriately into array      [cheat363]
   Display array as a grid                 [cheat364]
   Close the input file                    [cheat365]
*/
   int    row,
          column,
          row_index,
          column_index ;
   char   grid [ROWS] [COLUMNS] ;

}
```

Figure 14.6

15

Type definitions

15.1 Fundamental data types

We have so far used a selection of the fundamental data types provided as part of the C language. The full list of C fundamental data types is

char	signed char	unsigned char
int	short	long
unsigned	unsigned short	unsigned long
float	double	long double

In addition to holding a character, a variable of type char may be used to hold a small integer value. Hence type char has alternative forms: signed char (the default, and so the same as char) and unsigned char. The ranges of integer values that may be stored in variables of these types are

char	−128 to 127
signed char	−128 to 127
unsigned char	0 to 255.

Variables of type short, int and long are used to hold signed integer numbers. The range of values that may be contained in such variables is dependent upon the computer used. The ranges of values an ordinary personal computer would typically allow for variables of these types are

int	−32 768 to 32 767
short	−32 768 to 32 767
long	−2 147 483 648 to 2 147 483 647

Variables of type unsigned short, unsigned and unsigned long are used to hold unsigned integer numbers. On a typical personal computer system, variables of these types would have the following value ranges:

```
unsigned           0 to 65 535
unsigned short     0 to 65 535
unsigned long      0 to 4 294 967 295
```

Variables of type float, double and long double are used to hold real numbers. Again, their minimum and maximum values will depend on the computer system being used. All floating types allow for very small and very large numbers, so large that it is usual to represent them in floating point notation. Typically, variables of these types have the following ranges:

```
float          3.4E–38 to 3.4E+38
double         1.7E–308 to 1.7E+308
long double    3.4E–4932 to 1.1E+4932
```

We have also seen and used array variables. Arrays are not fundamental data types; rather, they are classified as derived types because they are derived from fundamental types.

With such a wide variety of fundamental data types and the ability to derive types for use as arrays, it might seem that a programmer has sufficient for most purposes. However, it is often necessary for a programmer to define a data type for a specific purpose within a program. C provides the typedef mechanism for this.

15.2   The use of typedef

typedef allows the programmer, in effect, to define new data types by associating a specific type to an identifier. Consider the following examples.

```
typedef int   PENCE ;
typedef int   KILOMETRES,
              MILES ;
typedef char LETTER ;
typedef int   TABLE [100] ;
```

In the first example we are declaring that we will use variables of type PENCE. Such variables will be used in exactly the same way as for integers. But by declaring and then using variables of type PENCE we will be associating the idea of processing a monetary value with such variables, and so the program will be that much more readable. We use upper-case for type identifiers as a standard in the same way as we did for symbolic constants.

In the second example we are declaring two types, KILOMETRES and MILES. We can declare variables of these types such as

```
KILOMETRES metric_distance ;
MILES      imperial_distance,
           journey_length ;
```

In the third example, we allow variables with the same properties as those of type char but with the more specific type name of LETTER to be declared.

Finally, the fourth example defines the type TABLE, which is an array of one hundred elements of type int. This will allow us to declare variables such as

```
TABLE exam_results ;
```

So the variable exam_results is an array of one hundred integer numbers and is equivalent to:

```
int exam_results [100] ;
```

Interestingly, we can use our new type definitions in further typedef statements. For example,

```
typedef int TABLE [100] ;
typedef TABLE TWO_DIM_TABLE [50] ;
```

This defines the type TWO_DIM_TABLE as 50 elements of the type TABLE. So we can declare a variable to hold a two-dimensional table by

```
TWO_DIM_TABLE school_results ;
```

This is equivalent to

```
int school_results [50] [100] ;
```

The main advantage of being able to define our own data types is that our declarations can now be more meaningful to the human reader and conceptually more appropriate to the programmer. There is one other fundamental data type, the *enumerated type* which helps in this way and allows us great flexibility in modelling values of variables in a meaningful way.

15.3   Enumerated types

Suppose we have five examinations at the end of a year, we could designate them by integers 1 to 5, or even by codes, such as examination subject codes. A program to manipulate examination results would use the integer designation for identification purposes, but this may require the programmer or anybody reading the source code to remember which subject is associated with each integer. (What if there were one hundred exams and one hundred codes to remember?) The program would be more readable if we could use the subject names.

C allows us to invent a data type by specifying the entire list of possible values, such values being any meaningful names we like. For example:

```
enum subject {programming, english, maths, french,
              computing} ;
enum days_of_week {Monday, Tuesday, Wednesday, Thursday,
                   Friday, Saturday, Sunday} ;
enum colours {red, yellow, blue} ;
enum units {centimetre, metre, kilometre} ;
```

Here, we have declared types such that a variable of type enum subject may have any of the five possible values indicated, a variable of type enum days_of_week may have any of the seven possible values indicated, and enum colours and enum units have three values each. Notice that the list of values of an enumerated type is bounded by braces rather than parentheses.

We can now declare variables as follows:

```
enum subject exam ;
enum days_of_week day ;
```

and then we could assign values associated with each of these types as follows:

```
exam = maths ;
day = Sunday ;
```

It is important to understand that enum subject is a data type defined by the programmer and that exam is a variable of that type, just as when declaring

```
int counter ;
```

we are specifiying that counter is a variable of the data type int provided by the C language.

We regard the names of values listed in the declaration of an enumerated type as constants of that type in the sense that we can use them in assignment statements, but the following are not allowed:

```
exam = 1 ;
day = programming ;
```

We must not confuse the values of an enumerated type with variables; programming is not a variable, rather it is a possible value of a variable of type enum subject and should only be used with variables of type enum subject.

The relational operators can be used with enumerated variables and values. The order is determined by the sequence in which the values are listed in the definition. For example, programming < maths.

We could even use the constant values in for statements, for example,

```
for (exam = programming ; exam <= computing ; ++ exam)
for (day = Monday ; day <= Friday ; ++ day)
```

or in switch statements,

```
switch (exam)
   {
   case programming  : exam_mark = exam_mark * 10 ;
                       break ;
   default           : exam_mark = exam_mark / 10 ;
   }
switch (day)
   {
   case Saturday   :
   case Sunday     : pay = rate * 2 * hours ;
                     break ;
   case Wednesday : pay = rate * hours / 2 ;
                     break ;
   default         : pay = rate * hours ;
   }
```

Consider the program in Fig. 15.1 that reads an examination results file with each line containing a student's name, followed by the examination and the coursework mark for each of the five subjects taken by the class, and calculates the total mark for each student from the weighted averages for each subject.

Notice that for an integer variable count, ++ count means the next integer value which is the same as 'add 1 to the value of count'. In this program we have used ++ exam, which must be interpreted as the next value in the declaration of enum subject. In this case, 'add 1 to the value of exam' would be meaningless.

In C it is not possible to read or write an enumerated type directly. For example,

```
printf ("%d", programming) ;
```

would not output 'programming'. It would output the position programming has in the enumerated list, namely 0. If we wished to achieve the effect implied by the above printf statement we would have to program it explicitly:

```
if (exam == programming)
   printf ("programming") ;
```

Exercises

1. Refer to Fig. 15.1. If you were to rewrite it without using enumerated types, what programming objective would be more difficult to achieve?
2. A university has faculties of Science, Medicine, Law and Engineering.
   (i) Write a declaration for the variable faculty by first defining an appropriate enumerated type.
   (ii) Write a program fragment to read a character from an input file, which could be S, M, L or E, and assign the corresponding value to faculty.

```
/* Output total of weighted averages for each student */
#include <stdio.h>
#include <string.h>
main ()
{
/* Description  ...... 
   Prepare input file and read first student name
   WHILE not end of file
      Process one set of marks
      Read next student name
   Close the input file
*/

   enum subject {programming, english, maths, french, computing} ;

   enum   subject exam ;
   int    exam_mark,
          cw_mark ;
   float mean,
          total ;
   char   student_name [10] ;
   FILE *exam_file = fopen ("examfile.dat", "r") ;

   fscanf (exam_file, "%s", student_name) ;
   while (strcmp (student_name, "ZZZZZZZZ") != 0)
      {
      total = 0 ;
      for (exam = programming ; exam <= computing ; ++ exam)
         {
         fscanf (exam_file, "%d%d", &exam_mark, &cw_mark) ;
         switch (exam)
            {
            case programming :
            case computing   :  mean = exam_mark * 0.6 +
                                   cw_mark * 0.4 ;
                                break ;
            case maths       :  mean = exam_mark * 0.8 +
                                   cw_mark * 0.2 ;
                                break ;
            default          :  mean = exam_mark * 0.9 +
                                   cw_mark * 0.1 ;
            }
         total = total + mean ;
         }
      printf ("%10s %.1f\n", student_name, total) ;
      fscanf (exam_file, "%s", student_name) ;
      }
   fclose (exam_file) ;
}
```

Figure 15.1

```
/* Compute weekly pay for an hourly-paid employee */
#include <stdio.h>
main ()
{
/* Description  ......
   Prompt for and read basic hourly rate
   Prompt for hours worked
   FOR each day of the week
      Read and process hours worked
   Output wages
*/
   float base_rate,
         rate,
         wages = 0.0 ;
   int   loop_control,
         hours ;

   printf ("Enter the basic hourly rate : ") ;
   scanf ("%f", &base_rate) ;
   printf ("Enter the hours worked for Monday through Sunday\n") ;
   for (loop_control = 1 ; loop_control <= 7 ; ++ loop_control)
      {
      scanf ("%d", &hours) ;
      if (loop_control <= 5)
         rate = base_rate ;
      else if (loop_control == 6)
         rate = base_rate * 1.5 ;
      else
         rate = base_rate * 2 ;
      wages += hours * rate ;
      }
   printf ("Wages for the week : %.2f\n", wages) ;
}
```

Figure 15.2

3. Amend the program given in Fig. 15.2 (and on the course disk as EX1503.C) to take advantage of the enumerated type facilities described in this chapter to make the code more readable.

4. Rewrite the following declarations taken from the program in Fig. 14.2 by defining three new types, one for the two-dimensional array and one each for variables associated with students and papers.

```
int  marks [STUDENTS] [PAPERS] = { 0 } ;
int  student_index,
     paper_index,
     student_total,
     student_number,
     paper_number ;
```

16

Structures and unions

16.1 Structures

We have already come across the idea of a record as a collection of components of information relating to a single object. For example, a record from a personnel file might include the following five fields for each person: surname, forename, date of birth, sex, marital status.

A record type in C is called a `struct` and is specified by defining an identifier and type for each of its fields (called *members*) between braces. For example,

```
struct date
    {
    int day,
        month,
        year ;
    } ;
struct student
    {
    char name [20] ;
    int  age ;
    char sex ;
    } ;
```

Here we have declared a `struct` type with a name `date` (called a `tag` in C) that has three members: day, `month` and `year`. Also, the `struct` type `student` has three members: name, `age` and `sex`. We can now declare variables of these `struct` types, for example,

Figure 16.1

```
struct date today,
            next_eclipse ;
struct date holidays [5] ;
struct student first_student,
            last_student ;
```

Each variable can be visualized as a box divided into components named by the members, as illustrated in Fig. 16.1.

As mentioned in the previous chapter, the reader should understand that struct date and struct student are data types defined by the programmer; today and first_student are variables of these types respectively. The tags date and student should not be used as variables.

We can declare structs without using a tag; the declaration is followed immediately by variable declarations of that type. For example, the variables first_student and last_student could be declared as

```
struct
    {
    char name [20] ;
    int  age ;
    char sex ;
    } first_student, last_student ;
```

Notice that in this case we have listed the variables after the closing brace but before the terminating semicolon. While this is a convenient shorthand, it does mean that we cannot declare other variables of this type later on in our program.

To refer to an individual member of a struct we use the *member access operator* '.' (full-stop). This allows us to use members in a program in exactly the same way as variables of the same type. For example, today.month selects the member month of the struct variable today (value 4 in Fig. 16.1). Now we can refer to members in assignment statements or function calls. For example,

```
next_eclipse.year = 1996 ;
first_student.age = 32 ;
prime_of_life = last_student.age ;
strcpy (first_student.name, "Brown") ;
```

```
/* Example program using structs for an employee record */
#include <stdio.h>
    typedef char STRING12 [12] ;
    struct date
        {
        int day,
            month,
            year ;
        } ;
    enum   job_status {manager, director, salesman, worker} ;
    struct person
        {
        STRING12 surname,
                 forename ;
        struct   date birth_date ;
        enum     job_status job ;
        } ;

main ()
{
/* Description ......
    For each employee in turn
        Read employee data into record
        Determine if suitable for promotion to manager
            and update record as appropriate
        Output the revised record
*/

    struct person employee ;
    int    counter ;
    struct person get_employee () ;
    void   display_employee (struct person) ;

    for (counter = 0 ; counter < 5 ; ++ counter)
        {
        employee = get_employee () ;
        if ((employee.job != manager) &&
            (employee.job != director) &&
            (employee.birth_date.year < 1970))
            employee.job = manager ;
        display_employee (employee) ;
        }
}

/* Function to get employee details from keyboard */
struct person get_employee ()
{
    struct person temp ;
    char   job_code ;
```

Figure 16.2

```
    printf ("Enter forename and surname : ") ;
    scanf ("%s%s", temp.forename, temp.surname) ;
    printf ("Enter date of birth and job status : ") ;
    scanf ("%d%d%d%c", &temp.birth_date.day,
        &temp.birth_date.month, &temp.birth_date.year,
        &job_code) ;
    switch (job_code)
        {
        case 'M' : temp.job = manager ;
                    break ;
        case 'D' : temp.job = director ;
                    break ;
        case 'S' : temp.job = salesman ;
                    break ;
        case 'W' : temp.job = worker ;
                    break ;
        }
    return temp ;
}

/* Function to display employee */
void display_employee (struct person an_employee)
{
    printf ("Forename and surname : %s %s\n",
        an_employee.forename, an_employee.surname) ;
    printf ("Date of birth : %d/%d/%d\n",
        an_employee.birth_date.day, an_employee.birth_date.month,
        an_employee.birth_date.year) ;
    printf ("Job status : ") ;
    switch (an_employee.job)
        {
        case manager   : printf ("manager\n") ;
                        break ;
        case director  : printf ("director\n") ;
                        break ;
        case salesman  : printf ("salesman\n") ;
                        break ;
        case worker    : printf ("worker\n") ;
                        break ;
        }
}
```

Figure 16.2 Continued.

Thus an individual member of a struct may have its value changed while the values of all other members are left unchanged.

We may also use the whole of a struct in assignment statements or as arguments in function calls. For example,

```
today = next_eclipse ;
```

copies the whole of the `struct  next_eclipse` into the `struct  today` and is possible because the two structs are of identical type. It is equivalent to, but better than,

```
today.day = next_eclipse.day ;
today.month = next_eclipse.month ;
today.year = next_eclipse.year ;
```

Let us now consider a more extensive example. Please examine the program shown in Fig. 16.2, which uses structs for an employee record.

The global declarations define the data type `struct  person`. The fourth member, `job`, is a variable of the enumerated type `job_status`, which allows for four values that represent certain job titles. The first two members of this `struct` are 12-character strings to hold a surname and a forename. The member `birth_date` is itself a `struct` variable, so it has members of its own. When we access such members we will need to use two member access operators. Since the `struct  person` has members with types `struct  date` and `enum job_status`, those two types have to be declared before `struct person`.

The function `main` has an interesting set of declarations:

```
struct person employee ;
int     counter ;
struct person get_employee () ;
void    display_employee (struct person) ;
```

The first declares the variable `employee` as a `struct` named `person`. The integer `counter` will be used in a `for` loop to deal with each of the five employees. The next two declarations are function prototypes; we recognize them as such by the parentheses. The first function `get_employee` takes no arguments and returns a result that is a `struct` of type `person`. The second takes a `struct` of type `person` as its argument and has no result, as indicated by the keyword `void`.

The remainder of `main` consists of a loop within which we have

```
employee = get_employee () ;
```

The `get_employee` function is called and returns a result that is assigned to the variable `employee`.

Then there is a single `if` statement that determines if the job status of the employee is to be changed.

```
if ((employee.job != manager) &&
    (employee.job != director) &&
    (employee.birth_date.year < 1970))
    employee.job = manager ;
```

The `if` statement sets the job status to manager as long as the current status is neither manager nor director, and the year of birth is before 1970. In the compound condition of this statement we access the member `job` using the member access operator, hence `employee.job`. The member `year` is a member of `birth_date` which in turn is a member of `employee`. In this case we need two member access operators, so we write `employee.birth_date.year`.

Finally we have

```
display_employee (employee) ;
```

The function `display_employee` is called and takes as its argument the variable `employee`.

The function `get_employee` has a variable `temp` that is of type `struct person`. This is used in the `scanf` statements where data are read into its members. Notice the second of these:

```
scanf ("%d%d%d%c", &temp.birth_date.day,
    &temp.birth_date.month, &temp.birth_date.year,
    &job_code) ;
```

Again we see the necessity to use two member access operators when accessing the members of `birth_date`. The `switch` statement is necessary to convert a single-character job code into an equivalent value of the enumerated type variable `job`.

```
switch (job_code)
   {
   case 'M' : temp.job = manager ;
              break ;
   case 'D' : temp.job = director ;
              break ;
   case 'S' : temp.job = salesman ;
              break ;
   case 'W' : temp.job = worker ;
              break ;
   }
```

The function `display_employee` uses similar concepts to those already described in `get_employee`, but note the use of the enumerated type variable `an_employee.job` as the expression in the switch statement.

In the sample program just explained we have seen a simple example of a data structure in which we have a structure (`date`) as part of another structure (`person`). A data structure may be regarded as an organized collection of data. Arrays and `structs` are types of data structure with their own particular properties. The fact that components of arrays and `structs` may themselves be structured allows us to build up data structures of some complexity.

For example, in the above program, if it had been necessary to store all five records in an array, then we would declare `employee` as an array of five `structs` (each with the structure defined in `person`):

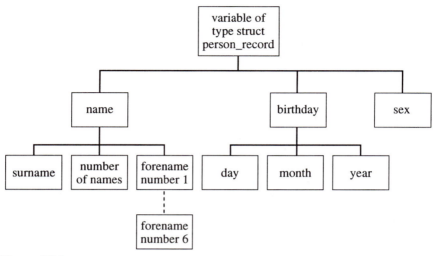

Figure 16.3

```
struct person employee [5] ;
```

We will now need to use an index to access each element of this array, that is the individual employee details. Thus, `employee [0].surname` and `employee [3].birthdate.year` would be used to access the surname of the first employee and the year of birth of the fourth employee respectively.

Data could be read into the array by means of a loop:

```
for (counter = 0 ; counter < 5 ; ++ counter)
    employee [counter] = get_employee () ;
```

The diagram given in Fig. 16.3, on the other hand, illustrates that an array, `forenames`, could be used within a `struct`.

This could be modelled by means of the following declarations:

```
#define MAX_NAMES 6 ;
typedef char STRING10 [10] ;
struct fullname
    {
    STRING10 surname ;
    int      number_of_names ;
    STRING10 forenames [MAX_NAMES] ;
    } ;
struct date
    {
    int day,
        month,
        year ;
```

```
    } ;
struct person_record
    {
    struct fullname name ;
    struct date birthday ;
    char    sex ;
    } ;
```

Note that surname, day, and sex are examples of elementary members, while name and birthday are examples of grouped members.

Given the declaration

```
struct person_record manager ;
```

we could now assign values to each elementary member of manager by means of

```
strcpy (manager.name.surname, "Gilbert") ;
strcpy (manager.name.forenames [1], "Anne") ;
strcpy (manager.name.forenames [2], "Kathryn") ;
manager.name.number_of_names = 2 ;
manager.birthday.day = 1 ;
manager.birthday.month = 3 ;
manager.birthday.year = 1950 ;
manager.sex = 'F' ;
```

16.2 Unions

A union is a derived type that is declared in a similar way to a struct. The crucial difference is that a union's members share the same storage area. For example, we might declare the following union and an associated variable number:

```
union any_number
    {
    int    integer_value ;
    float real_value ;
    } ;
union any_number number ;
```

We can now use the variable number to contain either an integer or a real number. For example, we might write:

```
number.real_value = 23.456 ;
```

or,

```
number.integer_value = 23 ;
```

Notice that we access the appropriate member using the member access operator. As the same storage is used for `number.real_value` and `number.integer_value` it is up to the user to interpret the stored values correctly.

We can use a `union` as part of a larger data structure. Consider the following small example:

```
union class
    {
    char   description [30] ;
    int    productivity ;
    } ;
struct production_record

    {
    char   data_type ;
    union class sub_field ;
    } ;

struct production_record item ;
```

Here we have first declared the `union` type `class` that will allow us to store either a 30 character string or an integer value. This is used in the `struct` `production_record`, which also contains a member of type `char` that may be used to contain a code D if the `sub_field` member is to be interpreted as a string, or P if it is to used as an integer. So we might write the following as part of a program:

```
printf ("Enter type of data followed by value: ") ;
scanf ("%c", &item.data_type) ;
if (item.data_type == 'D')
    scanf ("%s", item.sub_field.description) ;
else if (item.data_type == 'P')
    scanf ("%d", &item.sub_field.productivity) ;
else
    printf ("\nInvalid data type") ;
```

Exercises

1. Refer to Fig. 16.1 and state, where possible, the current values for the following:
    (i) `today.day`
    (ii) `next_eclipse.year`
    (iii) `day.next_eclipse`
    (iv) `date.year`.

2. With reference to the data structure illustrated in Fig. 16.3 and declared as the `struct person_record` in the text, a table of the above records could be declared as

   ```
   struct person_record person_table [NUMBER_OF_PEOPLE] ;
   ```

   (i) How would you access the record of the fifth person in the table?

   (ii) How would you access the third forename of the tenth person in the table?

3. (i)   Write the declarative part of a C program for storing the following details in `struct` variables `one_part` and `second_part`:

   (a) the part number – an integer

   (b) the part name – 9 characters

   (c) the price – a real number.

   (ii) Write the program fragment that gives the values 20 SOCKET 4.12 to `one_part`, then assigns these data to `second_part`.

   (iii) Write the program fragment that tests the part number of `one_part`; if it is less than 25 the price is doubled, otherwise it is trebled. Output the data from `second_part` with each field on a separate line.

4. Design and write a suitable data structure for storing the following payroll details:

   (i)   the works number – an integer;

   (ii) the employee's grade – a single letter;

   (iii) management code – a single character = T for true (is a manager) or F for false.

   Hence, design and write a complete program that reads each of four records from the file EX1604.DAT and displays each record as follows on the screen:

   ```
   WORKS NO. 999 GRADE x MANAGER
   ```

   or

   ```
   WORKS NO. 999 GRADE x NOT A MANAGER
   ```

   A line of data in EX1604.DAT is of the form:

   works no. followed by at least 1 space

   grade

   T or F

   If you need help in writing this program, an outline design is available in EX1604.C with appropriate cheats.

5. Write the declaration part of a C program to set up a data structure for storing the following details on no more than twenty cities:

   (i)   Name – up to twenty characters

   (ii) Code – a character

   (iii) Population – an integer.

   How would you access the name of the fifth city?

6. (i) Write a C data structure for storing the following details of a group of no
        more than thirty people:
       (a) Full name which is split into:
           surname – up to 20 characters;
           initials – up to 4 characters.
       (b) Date of joining the firm comprising:
           day – integer;
           month – integer;
           year – integer.
   (ii) Write code to assign values to:
       (a) the full name of the sixth person in the group;
       (b) the surname of the fourth person;
       (c) the month that the tenth person joined the firm;
       (d) the date that the twelfth person joined the firm.

17

Files

17.1 Streams

We have already discussed the use of files and the associated C functions. For example, we have used `fscanf`, `fprintf`, `fopen` and `fclose`. We now look at this area in a little more detail.

Input and output to any device, whether it be the monitor screen or a disk file, are viewed by the input and output part of the C system as a *flow* (or *stream*) of characters or a flow (or stream) of bytes. The system provides certain translations and provides access to parts of the stream of data (for example, an integer number) without the programmer being concerned with physical aspects of the device from which the data come or to which they go.

There are two types of data stream supported by C, text streams and binary streams. We will concern ourselves primarily with the former. In essence, a text stream is a file that we can create with a normal editor and one we can display on the screen using a standard listing command (TYPE in MS-DOS, for example). In such files we do not see certain characters such as new line characters. In binary streams all such characters are visible and must be catered for explicitly. For example, the new line is represented by \n in a text stream and is dealt with as one character. In fact, it is two ASCII characters and must be dealt with as two characters in a binary stream.

17.2 Input and output functions

As we have seen, when we wish to write to or read from a file, we must associate a particular file name with an identifier called a file pointer. For example,

```
FILE *inp_file ;
```

would declare the file pointer `inp_file`. The definition of the type `FILE` is contained within the standard header file `stdio.h`. It is, in fact, a structure that has a number of members containing information about a text stream; we do not need to concern ourselves with its details.

We use the function `fopen` to open a stream for input or output and link it to a specific file. For example,

```
inp_file = fopen ("ex1001.dat", "r") ;
```

Here `inp_file` will be given the value of a file pointer for the file known to the operating system as `ex1001.dat`. We can combine the declaration of the file pointer and the `fopen` by

```
FILE *inp_file = fopen ("ex1001.dat", "r") ;
```

The first argument to `fopen` is a string constant or string variable giving any file name that is valid to the operating system. However, if a path containing the '\' character is specified, for example, `A:\EXERCISE\EX1001.DAT` in MS-DOS, it should be noted that the '\' character should be repeated so that it is not interpreted as a control character. Hence we would write the string constant `"A:\\EXERCISE\\EX1001.DAT"`.

The second argument to `fopen` is a string constant that indicates the input/output mode. In our example, `"r"` means open an existing file for reading. The full list of modes is given in Fig. 17.1.

If an attempt is made to open a file for reading, mode `"r"` or `"r+"`, and the file does not exist, then the value returned to the file pointer will be `NULL`. It would be

---

```
"r"     open an existing text file for reading
"w"     create a text file for writing
"a"     append to an existing or create a new text file for
        writing
"r+"    open an existing text file for reading or writing
"w+"    create a text file for reading or writing
"a+"    append to an existing or create a new text file for
        reading or writing

"rb"    open an existing binary file for reading
"wb"    create a binary file for writing
"ab"    append to an existing or create a new binary file for
        writing
"r+b"   open an existing binary file for reading or writing
"w+b"   create a binary file for reading or writing
"a+b"   append to an existing or create a new binary file for
        reading or writing
```

Figure 17.1

good programming practice to test for NULL when opening input files. For example we could write:

```
FILE *inp_file = fopen ("ex1001.dat", "r") ;
if (inp_file == NULL)
    {
    printf ("File ex1001.dat does not exist\n") ;
    exit (1) ;
    }
```

One reason we should test for a file's existence is that if it does not exist then an attempt to read data from the file will cause a run-time error. The function exit, found in stdlib.h, causes normal program termination and passes the argument value to the calling environment (that is, the operating system).

We have seen that when writing to a file we may use the general purpose function fprintf. We use the same arguments for fprintf as for printf, except that we must specify the file pointer as the first argument for fprintf. For example,

```
FILE *results = fopen ("answer.txt", "w") ;

fprintf (results, "Answer is %d %s\n", answer,
    unit_string) ;
```

In addition to the fprintf function, there are a number of other functions provided by C for dealing with character output. We will now discuss two of them, fputc and fputs.

The function fputc may be used to output one character at a time to a file. For example,

```
char letter = 'Z' ;
FILE *alphabet_file = fopen ("letters.txt", "w") ;

fputc (letter, alphabet_file) ;
```

The first argument to fputc is the character to be output, and the second is the file pointer. If the call to fputc is successful it returns the value of the first argument; otherwise it returns the end-of-file value. We will discuss the end-of-file value later.

The function fputs may be used to output a string to a file. For example,

```
char  string10 [10] ;
FILE *string_file = fopen ("strings.txt", "w") ;

fputs ("We love Ada", string_file) ;
fputs (string10, string_file) ;
```

The first argument to fputs is the string to be output, and the second is the file pointer. A new line character is not automatically output after the string, neither is the terminating null character. If the call to fputs is successful it returns a non-negative value; otherwise, it returns the end-of-file value.

For general purpose reading from a file we use the function fscanf, which is similar to scanf except that it takes a file pointer as its first argument. For example,

```
FILE *inp_file = fopen ("figures.dat", "r") ;

fscanf (inp_file, "%d%s", &first, string10) ;
```

Again, C provides a number of character input functions. To illustrate this, we will discuss the fgetc, getchar and fgets functions.

We use the fgetc function to obtain a single character from the stream. For example,

```
char   letter ;
FILE *alphabet_file = fopen ("alpha.txt", "r") ;

letter = fgetc (alphabet_file) ;
```

The argument to fgetc is the file pointer. If the call is successful it returns the next character from the stream, otherwise it returns the end-of-file value.

If our input is from the keyboard, we could use the function getchar. This is similar to fgetc, but obviously does not need a file pointer as an argument. For example,

```
letter = getchar () ;
```

The function fgets may be used to read a string from a file. For example,

```
char   string10 [10] ;
FILE *string_file = fopen ("strings.txt", "r") ;

fgets (string10, 10, string_file) ;
```

The first argument to fgets is the identifier of the string, the second is the maximum number of characters that will be accepted into the string, and the third is the file pointer. The function will get characters from the input stream and place them in a character buffer until either a new line is read, or the end of the file is reached or the maximum number of characters minus one have been read. If the input was terminated by a new line it becomes part of the string. The null character is then appended. In Chapter 8 we noted that when using fscanf to read strings we could not input spaces and there was always the possibility of inputting more characters than the specified size of the string; fgets can obviously be used to overcome these problems. If the call to fgets is successful it returns the string, otherwise the function result is the end-of-file value.

17.3 End of file

The end-of-file value is an implementation defined constant called EOF (normally having the value −1). We may use it after calling the functions fputc, fputs, fgetc and fgets described above. For example,

```
letter = fgetc (alphabet_file) ;
if (letter == EOF)
    printf ("No more characters in alphabet file\n") ;
```

Another way of detecting the end of an input file is by invoking the function feof which takes the file pointer as its argument and returns a non-zero value if the end of the file has been reached, otherwise it returns zero. For example,

```
int    number ;
FILE *inp_file = fopen ("inp.dat", "r") ;

fscanf (inp_file, "%d", &number) ;
while (feof (inp_file) == 0)
    {
    printf ("%d\n", number) ;
    fscanf (inp_file, "%d", &number) ;
    }
```

If when fscanf is called there are no data to place in number (that is, we have reached end of file) an end-of-file indicator for the file is set and associated with the file pointer (inp_file). It is this indicator that is tested by feof in order to return the appropriate value.

Hence if we have a completely empty file, the first call to fscanf will cause the end-of-file indicator for inp_file to be set; this will be tested by the call to feof in the while statement and consequently the body of the loop will not be entered at all.

If there was just one numeric value in the file, this will be placed in number by the first fscanf and the end-of-file for inp_file will remain unset. Then, when feof is called for the first time in the while statement, zero will be returned and the body of the loop entered, and the printf and fscanf statements will be executed. Now, because there are no more data in the file, the call to fscanf will set the end-of-file indicator for inp_file and consequently, when feof is called for the second time, a non-zero value will be returned and the loop will be terminated.

When reading into an integer variable from an input file containing a single value followed by the invisible newline marker, the second call to fscanf will set the end-of-file indicator. On the other hand, when reading a single character variable from the same file, the third call to fscanf or fgetc would result in end-of-file being set. This is because the newline marker is read as a character and then on the third call there are no further character data to be read.

Let us now consider a program that uses some of the above-mentioned functions to display the contents of any text file. See Fig. 17.2.

```
/* A program to display the contents of any text file */
#include <stdio.h>
main ()
{
/* Description  ......
    DO
        Obtain filename and attempt to open file
    WHILE file not opened
    Read first line as a string
    WHILE not end of file
        Display a line
        Get the next line
    Close file
*/
    char  line [81] ;
    char  filename [30] ;
    FILE *inp_file ;

    do
        {
        printf ("Enter file name : ") ;
        scanf ("%s", filename) ;
        inp_file = fopen (filename, "r") ;
        if (inp_file == NULL)
            printf ("File %s does not exist\n", filename) ;
        }
    while (inp_file == NULL) ;
    fgets (line, 81, inp_file) ;
    while (feof (inp_file) == 0)
        {
        printf ("%s", line) ;
        fgets (line, 81, inp_file) ;
        }
    fclose (inp_file) ;
}
```

Figure 17.2

Notice that the user of the program must eventually enter a valid file name. The do-while loop will continue to prompt for and expect a file name as input until the call to fopen has been satisfied. Also, recall that calls to fgets will return a newline character as part of the string if that is what terminates the string. Hence, we do not need to include a \n as part of the control string of the printf statement.

```
/* Takes the 'lowest' letter from each line of a text file */
#include <stdio.h>
#include <stdlib.h>
main ()
{
/* Description  ......
    Prepare to process input file              [cheat390]
    Get first character                        [cheat391]
    WHILE not end of file                      [cheat392]
        Initialize lowest letter = Z           [cheat393]
        WHILE not end of line                  [cheat394]
            Store lowest letter so far         [cheat395]
            Get next character                 [cheat396]
        Display lowest letter in line          [cheat397]
        Process end of line (get a character)  [cheat398]
    Close the input file                       [cheat399]
*/
    char lowest_letter,
         letter ;


}
```

Figure 17.3

Exercises

1. Refer to the description of fgets in Section 17.2 of this chapter. What is the difference between the results of the following two statements?
   (i) fscanf (file_pointer, "%s", string_variable) ;
   (ii) fgets (string_variable, 25, file_pointer) ;
2. An input file EX1702.DAT contains lines of letters of the alphabet. Write a program using the outline given in EX1702.C (see Fig. 17.3) that determines for each line of the file the letter on that line that comes first in the alphabet. Write the results to the screen, one letter per line. For example, a file with the contents

   ON
   BOB

   would produce

   N
   B

   Your solution should test for NULL when opening the input file and stop the program with an appropriate terminating message if the file does not exist. Also, you should use the function fgetc in your program.
3. An input file EX1703.DAT consists of a long sentence, that is, characters ter-

minated by a full-stop. The sentence consists of a number of phrases, that is, characters terminated by a comma. For example,

```
ABC, VAV, XXV
V,   AD
EF.
```

Design and write a program that produces on the screen the following analysis:

```
PHRASE          NO. OF CHARACTERS
   1                  3
   2                  4
   3                  6
   4                  7
```

Note that 'no. of characters' should include spaces and new line characters but not the comma or full-stop. The program should stop with an appropriate message if the input file cannot be opened.

An outline design is available in EX1703.C with appropriate cheats.

4. Design and write a program to compare the contents of any two text files. The files should be compared line by line with a simple message being displayed, such as The following lines are different, followed by the contents of the two lines, whenever a line from the first file is not the same as a line from the second file. When the end of one (or both) of the files is reached the comparison is terminated and one of the following messages is displayed: Files are of unequal length., Files are the same length but different contents., or Files are the same..

See Fig. 17.2 for an example of how to prompt for a file name and then open that file for reading. If required, an outline design is available in EX1704.C with appropriate cheats.

18

Software units

18.1 The preprocessor

The complete C compilation system consists of a number of stages. The first stage evaluates preprocessor directives to include source code from elsewhere, establish symbolic constants, and, as we shall see in the next section, expand macro definitions.

Preprocessor directives start with #. We have already met a number of them, for example:

```
#include <stdio.h>
```

This causes the preprocessor to replace this line with the contents of the file called stdio.h found in the compiler's *include* directory. The angular brackets < > indicate to the preprocessor that the enclosed file name is to be found in the standard place for such files. This standard place will differ from compiler to compiler, but in most cases it will be a subdirectory called INCLUDE. The use of the file name extension .h is a convention to indicate header files. The header files provided by the C compilation system are readable; you may wish to examine stdio.h for example, but beware the fact that it is likely to contain advanced features of the C language that are beyond the scope of this text.

We can develop our own header files to contain, for example, our own function prototypes or type definitions. We may use them in our programs by writing

```
#include "myheader.h"
```

Notice that we now enclose the file name with quotation marks. This indicates to the preprocessor that the file is to be found either in the current directory or, if not in there, in other subdirectories specified by the compilation system.

Another commonly used directive is the #define directive. This can be used to define symbolic constants, which we have already described, or macros, as we shall see later. A symbolic constant is simply an identifier that can be used to represent some value or text. For example,

```
#define MAXIMUM 180
```

When MAXIMUM is written in a program that contains this #define directive, it is replaced with the value 180 by the preprocessor. Note that such identifiers are normally written in uppercase. This is not a rule of C, but a programming convention.

Normally, the #define directive is placed at the beginning of a program; but it does not have to be. If a #define directive is placed in the middle of a program, only the occurrences of the defined identifier appearing after the directive are replaced with its value.

Any occurrences of a #define identifier that appear in comments and quoted strings are protected and will not be translated. For example, if we had written

```
printf ("THE MAXIMUM IS %d", MAXIMUM) ;
```

then the second MAXIMUM would be converted to 180 but the first, being in a quoted string, would not.

In general, we use #define directives with symbolic constants to increase program readability. Meaningful identifiers can then be used in a program and they will consistently be interpreted as the value given to them. Further, if the program is changed, it is a lot easier to change a #define statement than every occurrence of a particular value.

We can also use #define to customize our programs. Because the preprocessor changes every relevant occurrence of a symbolic constant to its defined value, we can use it to invent our own syntax to replace that given to us. For example if we wished to use the BEGIN and END statements from the Pascal programming language instead of braces, we could write:

```
#define BEGIN {
#define END }
```

Then we could write:

```
while (token <= 99999)
   BEGIN
   printf ("Token value = %d\n", token) ;
   token = token * 5 ;
   END
```

The BEGIN would be replaced by { and the END by }, thus conforming to the syntax rules of C.

This is a very powerful tool, but like most powerful tools it can be misused.

18.2 Macros

We can use the #define directive to write macro definitions with parameters. For example, we might write:

```
#define SQR(x) ((x) * (x))
```

As we have seen with symbolic constants, each occurrence of SQR following the #define directive would be replaced by the defined string. The defined string in this case is parameterized; that is, it contains two occurrences of the character x. When SQR is used in the body of the program it must specify a value for x. For example,

```
printf ("%d\n", SQR (5)) ;
```

In this case the expansion of the macro SQR would be:

```
printf ("%d\n", ((5) * (5))) ;
```

In other words, the defined string is copied exactly into the program text but with the parameter x being replaced by the macro parameter 5.

In this example there appear to be superfluous parentheses. But they all need to be present to allow for a complete expression to replace the parameter x, as in the following example:

```
printf ("%d\n", SQR (5 - figure)) ;
```

which expands to:

```
printf ("%d\n", ((5 - figure) * (5 - figure))) ;
```

Without the parentheses, there is a danger of the resultant expression giving wrong results, owing to an unexpected order of evaluation.

The preprocessor does not do any validation of any macro expansion; it simply replaces a macro with its expansion including any parameters. Hence, it is possible to produce syntax errors in our C code unless care is taken with both the macro definition and its use in a program.

Once a macro has been defined, it can be incorporated in other macro definitions. For example, we can use the SQR macro to produce a CUBE macro:

```
#define CUBE(x) (SQR(x) * (x))
```

18.3 Writing large programs

When we are required to write large programs, it makes good sense to split the program into easily managed parts. We might decide to create our own header files in which we could put our function prototypes, any common typedef and struct definitions, and any macros or symbolic constants. We could then decide to create several C source files each containing just one or two functions. These

STUDENT ADMISSIONS
═══════════════════

1. B.Sc. Computer Studies
2. B.Sc. Software Engineering
3. Exit from system

Please enter 1, 2 or 3 then <Enter>:

Figure 18.1

source files could be written and compiled independently by one or more programmers. We might also be able to test the functions in one C source file
independently. In most cases we would have to write a simple function to invoke
the functions to be tested. Developing software in this manner can achieve the
following benefits:

1. Separate development of syntactically correct software components.
2. Separate concurrent development of related software components by more than
   one programmer.
3. The possibility of separate testing of software components. This may mean
   more thorough testing.
4. Construction and availability of software libraries.

Let us now consider the development of a program which, although small
enough to be described here, can be treated in the same way as a large program.
We are required to design and write a simple interactive program as a main
program function in one C source file and two other functions each in its own C
source file. The main program function offers a simple menu as shown in
Fig. 18.1.

If menu option 1 is selected, a function is called to read the file BSCCS.DAT
containing names of students accepted on that course. The names are displayed
allowing the screen to scroll. After all the names have been displayed a prompt is
displayed and once the user has responded control is returned to the menu.

If menu option 2 is selected another function is called to read the file
BSCSE.DAT containing names of students accepted on that course. Each name is
displayed in the middle of the screen, followed by a prompt asking if the user
wishes to continue. Control is returned to the menu if the user responds N to the
prompt or the end of file is reached.

Figure 18.2 contains the main menu function.

Notice the #include statement for the header file EX1801.H. This file will be
included in each of our C source files for this system. It would be built up as the
system is developed to contain #include statements of general use in the system
and function prototypes of the functions we develop. Figure 18.3 shows the final
contents of this header file.

```
/* Student admissions */
#include "ex1801.h"
main ()
{
/* Menu for student admissions */
/* Description  ......
    DO
        Display menu
        Accept user choice
        Call appropriate routine
    WHILE exit not selected
*/
    char user_choice ;

    do
        {
        printf ("\n              STUDENT  ADMISSIONS\n") ;
        printf ("              ===================\n") ;
        printf ("      1. B.Sc. Computer Studies\n") ;
        printf ("      2. B.Sc. Software Engineering\n") ;
        printf ("      3. Exit from system\n\n") ;
        printf ("Please enter 1, 2 or 3 then <Enter> : ") ;
        do
            {
            user_choice = getchar () ;
            getchar () ;              /* To skip new line char. */
            }
        while (! ((user_choice >= '1') && (user_choice <= '3'))) ;
        if (user_choice == '1')
            cs_student () ;           /* B.Sc. C.S. function */
        else if (user_choice == '2')
            se_student () ;           /* B.Sc. S.E. function */
        }
    while (user_choice != '3') ;
}
```

Figure 18.2

```
/* Header file for student admissions */
#include <stdio.h>
#include <ctype.h>
void cs_student () ;
void se_student () ;
```

Figure 18.3

```
/* Function to deal with B.Sc. C.S. students */
#include "ex1801.h"
void cs_student ()
{
/* Description  ......
   Prepare file for processing and read first record
   WHILE not end of file
      Display name
      Read next record
   Prompt for exiting the screen
   Close input file
*/
   char  user_response ;
   char  name [15] ;
   FILE *bsccs = fopen ("bsccs.dat", "r") ;

   fgets (name, 15, bsccs) ;
   printf ("\n\n") ;
   while (feof (bsccs) == 0)
      {
      printf ("%s", name) ;
      fgets (name, 15, bsccs) ;
      }
   printf ("\nPress <Enter> to exit......") ;
   user_response = getchar () ;
   fclose (bsccs) ;
}
```

Figure 18.4

If we wanted to test the main program function before developing the other functions, we could put comment brackets around the two function calls. Of course, all that this would test is the layout of the menu. Alternatively, we could replace the two function calls with appropriate printf statements; this would then test whether or not these statements were being reached and executed.

The function for the first menu option contained in its own source file is shown in Fig. 18.4. This function could be tested separately by adding a main function at the end of the source file. For example,

```
main ()
{
cs_student () ;
}
```

Figure 18.5 shows the contents of the file that contains the function for the second menu option.

Here we have used the toupper function found in ctype.h; this converts a lower-case character to upper case. It is useful here because it allows the user to type in a response in either upper or lower case.

```
/* Function to deal with B.Sc. S.E. students */
#include "ex1801.h"
void se_student ()
{
/* Description  ......
   Prepare file for processing and read first record
   WHILE user does not quit and not end of file
       Display name
       Prompt for continuation and get user response
       Read next record
   Close input file
*/
   char   user_response = 'Y' ;
   char   name [15] ;
   FILE *bscse = fopen ("bscse.dat", "r") ;

   fgets (name, 15, bscse) ;
   while ((user_response == 'Y') && (feof (bscse) == 0))
       {
       printf ("\n\n%s\n\n", name) ;
       printf ("Do you wish to continue? (Y/N <Enter>) : ") ;
       do
           {
           user_response = toupper (getchar ()) ;
           getchar () ;                    /* To skip new line char. */
           }
       while ((user_response != 'Y') && (user_response != 'N')) ;
       fgets (name, 15, bscse) ;
       }
   fclose (bscse) ;
}
```

Figure 18.5

Again, this function could be tested separately by incorporating a simple main function as follows at the end of the file:

```
main ()
{
se_student () ;
}
```

Many computer systems provide useful utility programs, which facilitate the compilation and control of programming projects that involve a number of source files. In most cases this is referred to as a *make* utility and often uses a small set of commands, in a small file, that control the compilation of the program. Some systems integrate the development of programming projects, so that it may be unnecessary to use header files in quite the same way as we have done in our small program above. When you start building multi-file programs it will be necessary to investigate the facilities provided on your own computer system.

Exercises

1. Demonstrate the use of `#define` statements in declaring an array and then using a `for` statement to fill the array elements with the numbers 12 to 23 inclusive.

2. With reference to the macro definition of `SQR` in Section 18.2, what would be the expansion for the following line of code?

```
result = SQR (y + 8 / z) + x ;
```

3. Given the macro definition

```
#define CUBE(y)  SQR(y)*y
```

what expansion would be given for the following statement, and why would it be wrong?

```
error = 5 + CUBE (x + 3) ;
```

4. This question refers to the simple interactive program described in Section 18.3. Amend the menu program given in Fig. 18.2 (EX1801.C) to incorporate a new option:

```
3. H.N.D. Computer Studies
```

Write a new component that contains a function to read the file HNDCS.DAT and display all names in the file with a maximum of twelve per screen and a user continuation prompt at the foot of each screen (for example, `Press return to view the next screen:`).

The functions for menu options 1 and 2 are in EX1802.C and EX1803.C respectively. If you need them, an outline for the new function is available in EX1804.C with appropriate cheats; EX1805.C is provided as a new main program incorporating the new menu option and EX1805.H is provided as a new header file.

19

Dynamic data structures

19.1 Pointers

We have already met the concept of pointers in Chapter 10. Recall that if we wanted to change the values of the arguments of a function, then in the function call we passed across the addresses of variables. For example in the swap function, we used

```
swap (&first_number, &second_number) ;
```

In the function definition we specified the parameters as pointers to float variables:

```
void swap (float *first, float *second)
```

The type of an address of a float variable is known as a *pointer* to a float variable. We can declare pointers to data types by specifying the indirection operator * before the identifier. For example:

```
int *p_integer ;
```

declares a pointer variable p_integer, in which we can store the address of any int variable. So if we have declared an int variable number, we can store its address in p_integer by

```
p_integer = &number ;
```

This means that number can have its value changed, either directly by statements such as

```
number = 25 ;
```

or indirectly through the address of number held in p_integer by using the indirection operator:

```
*p_integer = 25 ;
```

Notice that p_integer holds the address of an integer variable, whereas *p_integer denotes, or points to, the store location associated with that variable.

We can use pointers of structs as well as of fundamental data types. Recall the struct date from Chapter 16:

```
struct date
   {
   int day,
       month,
       year ;
   } ;
```

If we wished to construct a function that takes such a struct as an argument and returns the date changed to that exactly three months later, we would pass the address of the struct. The function heading would be

```
void new_date (struct date *anniversary)
```

and the statements to manipulate the members of the struct would be of the form

```
(*anniversary).month += 3 ;
```

The parameter anniversary holds the address of the struct, so (*anniversary).month denotes the member month of the struct whose address is found in anniversary.

A simpler way of accessing the members of a struct from a pointer is provided by the member access operator (->). Instead of writing (*anniversary).month we can use the alternative syntax anniversary->month; again, this enables us to access the member month from the struct pointed to by anniversary.

Using pointers is an important way of accessing data structures, especially, as we shall see, when building data structures from dynamically allocated memory.

19.2 Stacks

A *static* data structure is a data structure that remains fixed in size throughout its lifetime and whose size we can always determine by examining its declaration in the program. For example, we have already used arrays and structs as static data structures.

Dynamic data structures, on the other hand, change in size during the execution of the program. Because of this we need a different way of referencing them. For

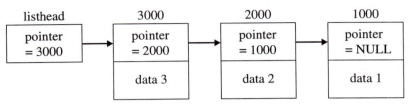

Figure 19.1

arrays we use an index of an element's fixed position as a reference. For dynamic structures we use a pointer.

The *stack* is the simplest type of dynamic data structure. In a stack each element is linked to the next, but access to the elements is restricted such that we may only add new elements at the top of the stack and take elements away from the top of the stack. We call this a *last-in-first-out* (often written as *LIFO*) structure, because the last element to be added to the list is the only one that is available. An allegory often used to explain a stack is that of a pile of trays in a self-service restaurant. Only the top tray is accessible. We may add a tray to the top and this becomes the new top tray, or we may remove a tray from the top, at which point the tray beneath becomes the top tray.

We can represent a stack in computer memory diagrammatically as in Fig. 19.1. Here, we have a *list head* or *stack pointer* that links us to the first element at the top of the stack, containing `data3` and a pointer to the next (second) element, which in turn contains `data2` and a pointer to the next (third) element containing `data1` and a pointer pointing to nowhere (represented by the word `NULL`). (Note that although the actual position in the computer's main memory is unknown to us, we will imagine the locations as addresses 3000, 2000 and so on. These addresses have no special significance, they are used purely to aid the illustration. In a computer the addresses could be a variety of different values.)

As we can see from Fig. 19.1, each element of the stack has two parts; one part contains the actual data and the other part contains a pointer to the next element. Thus, to define a dynamic data structure, we need a data structure that contains a pointer; in most cases this will be a `struct`. Hence we can define an element of the stack in Fig. 19.1 by:

```
struct element
    {
    struct element *next ;
    int     data ;
    } ;
```

Notice that the first member of the data type `struct element` is a pointer to a location of the same type.

We will also find it convenient to declare a data type that is a pointer to this struct:

```
typedef struct element *LINK ;
```

Since LINK is a pointer data type, we now declare pointer variables as, for example,

```
LINK a_pointer,
     b_pointer ;
```

Let us now construct a stack using C, given the declarations above. First, we need a pointer variable for the head of the list, called the list head or stack pointer. This is declared of type LINK, and we initialize it to NULL (at the start there is no stack so there is nothing to point to).

```
LINK listhead = NULL ;
```

To put an element on the stack, we first need to create the element using the standard function malloc (memory allocation) found in stdlib.h.

```
LINK newpointer ;
newpointer = malloc (sizeof (struct element)) ;
```

Here, we have declared a pointer variable called newpointer, then we have invoked malloc. The function malloc obtains memory from a part of the program's memory known as the *heap* and stores its address in newpointer. The amount of memory needed is defined by the argument to malloc; in this case this is computed by a call to the sizeof function with data type struct element as its argument. The result type of malloc is a generic pointer denoted by void *.

We now have two pointer variables listhead and newpointer with the latter being associated with a data structure of type struct element. We can visualize this situation by the diagram given as Fig. 19.2.

The next step is to assign some information to the new element. When dealing with members of a struct we have previously used variable_name.member_identifier as in employeerec.name. Thus

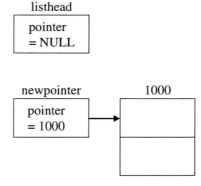

Figure 19.2

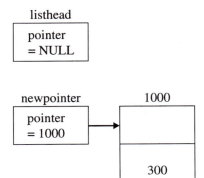

Figure 19.3

using this syntax, (*newpointer).data would access the member data of the struct whose address is given by newpointer. However, as we have mentioned above, there is an alternative, the 'arrow' member access operator (->). This emphasizes the fact that we are accessing the struct by a reference rather than by a name, that is, we are pointing to the struct. For example,

```
newpointer->data = 300 ;
```

gives a value of 300 to the member data in the struct referenced by (or pointed to by) newpointer->. We can show this by extending Fig. 19.2 to give Fig. 19.3.

We next need to establish a link between the list head and the first element in our stack, and also set the pointer next to NULL. As listhead contains NULL, we first assign its pointer contents to newpointer->next, then we update the contents of listhead with the pointer value of newpointer.

```
newpointer->next = listhead ;
listhead = newpointer ;
```

We can now further update our diagram to give the revised diagram shown in Fig. 19.4.

We now have a stack of one element! We could have referenced listhead directly without using newpointer. However, by taking this approach we have defined code which can be used repeatedly to build a complete stack. The same sequence of instructions is used to create additions to the beginning of the stack. For example, to put a data item of 200 at the head of the stack (that is, between listhead and data item 300) we adopt the following procedure:

1. Create a new element using malloc (that is, get some memory from the heap for the element).
2. Assign data to the element.
3. Make this element point to the next item (that is, put the pointer value currently in listhead into the member next).

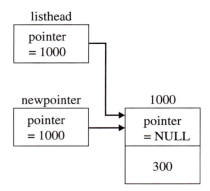

Figure 19.4

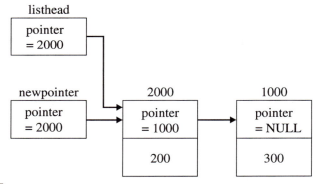

Figure 19.5

4. Make listhead point to the new element.

In C we would write:

```
newpointer = malloc (sizeof (struct element)) ;
newpointer->data = 200 ;
newpointer->next = listhead ;
listhead = newpointer ;
```

Now our diagram is as in Fig. 19.5.

Similarly, to put a new data item of 100 at the head of the stack, we would write the following C code:

```
newpointer = malloc (sizeof (struct element)) ;
newpointer->data = 100 ;
newpointer->next = listhead ;
listhead = newpointer ;
```

This gives the stack shown in Fig. 19.6.

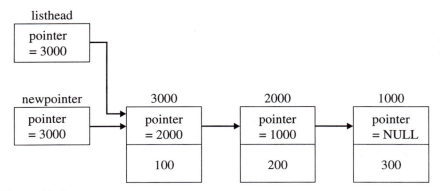

Figure 19.6

The above code gives the basic algorithm for adding a new data element to a stack; this is known as *pushing onto the stack*.

Taking an item off a stack is referred to as *popping* and is done on a *last-in-first-out* basis. To remove the top element from the stack in Fig. 19.6, we would adopt the following procedure:

1. Make a temporary variable point to the element currently at the head of the list.
2. Make `listhead` point to the next item in the stack.
3. Release the memory back to the heap using the temporary variable.

The corresponding code is

```
temp = listhead ;
listhead = listhead->next ;
free (temp) ;
```

The pointer variable `temp` is used to preserve a copy of the pointer value in `listhead`. We need it in a moment. Next the pointer in `listhead` is changed. Its new value is taken from the `next` pointer of the element it is currently pointing to. The effect of this is to make `listhead` point to the next element in the stack. In Fig. 19.6 `listhead` points to element 3000. This data element's `next` pointer contains a pointer to element 2000. If `listhead` is changed to contain the `next` pointer from element 3000, the effect will be that it will now point to element 2000.

The `free` function found in `stdlib.h` releases memory back to heap storage. Its argument is a pointer to some memory space. The memory space to be released is that of the element we have just taken off the stack. The pointer to this is the old value of `listhead`. That is why we saved a copy of `listhead` in `temp`.

Consider the program shown in Fig 19.7 that uses functions called `push` and `pop` to print out a list of names in reverse order. After the global declarations for the `struct name_rec` and a pointer type to the `struct` called `LINK`, we

```
/* Reads names file and pushes on to a stack, then pops all */
/* names off the stack printing the names in reverse order  */
#include <stdio.h>
#include <stdlib.h>
#include <string.h>
    struct name_rec
        {
        char name [10] ;
        struct name_rec *next ;
        } ;
    typedef struct name_rec *LINK ;
    LINK listhead = NULL ;

main ()
{
/* Description  ......
    Prepare to process file and read first name
    WHILE not end of file
        Push name on to stack
        Read next name
    WHILE not end of stack
        Pop name off stack
    Close the input file
*/
    char a_name [10] ;
    void push (char *) ;
    void pop () ;
    FILE *names = fopen ("names.dat", "r") ;

    fscanf (names, "%s", a_name) ;
    while (feof (names) == 0)
        {
        push (a_name) ;
        fscanf (names, "%s", a_name) ;
        }
    while (listhead != NULL)
        pop () ;
    fclose (names) ;
}

/* Function to Push item on to stack */
void push (char *this_name)
{
/* Description  ......
    Create new dynamic variable
    Assign data and link to list head
*/
    LINK newpointer ;

    newpointer = malloc (sizeof (struct name_rec)) ;
```

Figure 19.7

```
    if (newpointer == NULL)
        {
        printf ("No memory available\n") ;
        exit (1) ;
        }
    else
        {
        strcpy (newpointer->name, this_name) ;
        newpointer->next = listhead ;
        listhead = newpointer ;
        }
}

/* Function to Pop an item from the stack */
void pop ()
{
/* Description  ......
    Display item at head of list then change head pointer
*/
    LINK temp ;

    printf ("%s\n", listhead->name) ;
    temp = listhead ;
    listhead = listhead->next ;
    free (temp) ;
}
```

Figure 19.7 Continued.

have the pointer listhead initialized to NULL. The function main is simply two loops, one to control reading the names file and pushing names on to the stack by calling push, and the other to control the printing of the names in reverse order by popping from the stack until the stack is empty, that is, until listhead again points to nothing (has a value of NULL).

In Chapter 8 we noted that during the reading of string variables, for example,

```
scanf ("%s%s", street, town) ;
```

there was no need to include the & (indicating the address of the variable) before the variable. This is because arrays of characters are implemented in C as pointer data types. Consequently, when using strings as arguments in functions, we indicate the pointer type in the prototype and function definition. Note that the argument of push in Fig. 19.7 is a string and we have used the prototype

```
void push (char *) ;
```

and then the function definition

```
void push (char *this_name)
```

The function push introduces another feature we have yet to describe. If a call to malloc is unsuccessful (that is, it is unable to allocate memory), a NULL pointer value is returned. This is tested for in the function and the program is stopped by the exit statement. It is good programming practice to incorporate such a test when allocating memory.

The function pop uses the procedure described above and includes

```
printf ("%s\n", listhead->name) ;
```

Here, the name pointed to by listhead is printed. The first time pop is called this will be the last one added to the stack.

19.3   Queues

A *queue* is another simple form of dynamic data structure. In a queue we have two base pointers, a list head and a list tail. We need two because we add elements to the tail, but remove elements from the head. Just like an orderly queue at a bus stop, new arrivals go to the end of the queue, and the first to leave the queue (to board the bus) is the one at the head of the queue. A queue is said to be a *first-in-first-out* (*FIFO*) structure.

To form a queue structure, we first create pointers for the head and tail of the queue. We can represent this by the diagram in Fig. 19.8. Notice that to start with the value of both pointers is NULL.

When we wish to put an element into the queue, we put it at the tail of the queue; hence we must update the tail pointer to point to it. Also, if the element is

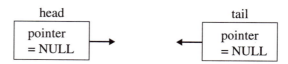

Figure 19.8

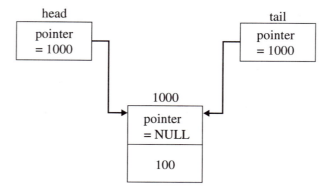

Figure 19.9

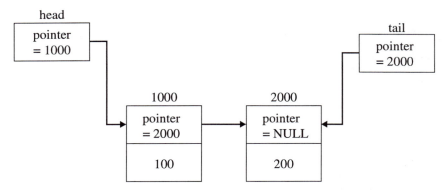

Figure 19.10

the first one in the queue, we must ensure that the head pointer is pointing to this element. The diagram given as Fig. 19.9 illustrates a queue with one element. Notice how both head and tail point to the one element, but the element itself has a NULL pointer.

When we add a second, or subsequent, element to the queue, we again put it at the rear. This means we must change the tail to point to this new element. Also, we link the new element to the one that precedes it in the queue by updating the predecessor's pointer. In this way the elements of a queue are linked so that we can always access every element starting at the head. Figure 19.10 shows the updated queue with two elements. Notice how the pointers in the tail and the predecessor have been updated.

Thus the algorithm for adding an item to the end of a queue is given by the following:

1. Create a new arrival using malloc.
2. Assign data to the new arrival.
3. Make this new arrival point nowhere.
4. If the queue is empty make the head point to the new arrival, otherwise make the predecessor point to the new arrival.
5. Make the tail point to the new arrival.

You might like to compare this with the procedure given in the previous section for putting a new element on the top of a stack.

Note that an element is removed from the front of a queue in exactly the same way as an element is taken off the top of a stack. The procedures for doing this are therefore basically the same.

Let us now consider a program that uses a queue structure. We will simulate a simple print spooling queue. First we will create a queue from a file of integers representing the size of print files in bytes. Then we will accept integer values from the keyboard to represent the sizes of new print jobs received or zero to signify that a job is to be taken off the queue. For each non-zero value accepted we

```
/* Updates a queue of print jobs */
#include <stdio.h>
#include <stdlib.h>
#include <ctype.h>
    struct job
       {
       struct job *next ;
       int    length ;
       } ;
    typedef struct job *LINK ;

    LINK   head = NULL,
           tail = NULL ;
    void add_item (int) ;

main ()
{
/* Description  ......
    First establish initial queue
    DO
        Get next job length
        IF a new item
           Put this item into queue
        ELSE IF an item left to remove
           Display head of queue
           Remove item from front of queue
        Prompt to continue
    WHILE input to process
*/
    int    input_length ;
    char   yes_no ;
    LINK   temp ;
    void create_queue () ;

    create_queue () ;
    do
       {
       printf ("\nEnter next job length <Enter>: ") ;
       scanf ("%d", &input_length) ;
       getchar () ;              /* Skip new line character */
       if (input_length != 0)
          add_item (input_length) ;
       else if (head != NULL)
          {
          printf ("Head of queue going off is : %d\n",
             head->length) ;
          temp = head ;
          head = head->next ;
          free (temp) ;
          }
       printf ("Any more? (Y/N <Enter>) : ") ;
       yes_no = toupper (getchar ()) ;
```

Figure 19.11

```
        getchar () ;                    /* Skip new line character */
        }
   while (yes_no == 'Y') ;
}

/* Function to add an item to the queue */
void add_item (int this_length)
{
/* Description  ......
   Build new item
   Add to end of queue
*/
   LINK new_arrival = malloc (sizeof (struct job)) ;

   if (new_arrival == NULL)
      {
      printf ("Not enough memory\n") ;
      exit (1) ;
      }
   else
      {
      new_arrival->length = this_length ;
      new_arrival->next = NULL ;
      if (head == NULL)
         head = new_arrival ;
      else
         tail->next = new_arrival ;
      tail = new_arrival ;
      }
}

/* Function to read jobs file and create queue */
void create_queue ()
{
/* Description  ......
   Open jobs file and read first job length
   WHILE not end of file
       Put job length in queue
       Read next job length
   Close the input file
*/
   int   input_length ;
   FILE *jobs = fopen ("jobs.dat", "r") ;

   fscanf (jobs, "%d", &input_length) ;
   while (feof (jobs) == 0)
      {
      add_item (input_length) ;
      fscanf (jobs, "%d", &input_length) ;
      }
   fclose (jobs) ;
}
```

Figure 19.11 Continued.

will add it to the back of the queue. When a value of zero is received, the item at the front of the queue is displayed and then removed from the queue. Figure 19.11 contains this program.

After the global declarations for the struct job and a pointer type to the struct called LINK, we have the pointers head and tail. Also, we have a global prototype for the function add_item. This is declared globally because it is used in both of the other functions of the program.

The function main first calls the create_queue function to establish the queue from the input file. The do-while loop that follows prompts the user for input then invokes the add_item function to add the new non-zero value to the queue. If a zero value is entered and the head pointer is not NULL (that is, the queue is not empty), the element at the head of the queue is displayed by using the head pointer, then this element is removed by changing the value of the head pointer to point to the next in the list and freeing the memory used by the removed element. This latter process is just as we saw for removing items from a stack.

The function add_item first attempts to get some memory from heap storage; if this is not possible the program is terminated. The C statements for putting a new element at the rear of the queue, corresponding to the algorithm given above, are now examined in detail.

```
new_arrival->length = this_length ;
new_arrival->next = NULL ;
```

Here we are assigning values to the two members of this job; this_length is obtained from the function's parameter, and we initialize the new pointer (in this case the member next) to NULL.

```
if (head == NULL)
   head = new_arrival ;
else
   tail->next = new_arrival ;
```

If we have an empty queue, the value of the head pointer will be NULL. So, we can establish if the queue is empty in this manner. If it is, we must change the value of the head pointer so that it points to the first element in the queue (new_arrival in our case). If there are already elements in the queue, we need to link the last element to the one we are adding. We do this by using the tail pointer because this points to the last element in the queue. The last element of the queue has a next pointer that will have a value of NULL, we change it to point to the new element (new_arrival).

```
tail = new_arrival ;
```

Finally, we update the tail pointer so that it now points to the new element.

The function create_queue is relatively straightforward in that it simply reads the input file and for each integer read it calls the function add_item.

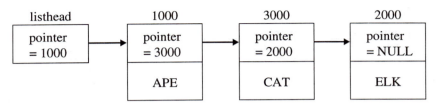

Figure 19.12

19.4   Ordered linked lists

A more general application of dynamic data structures occurs when the data items in a linked list are held in a specific order, that is, sorted on a key value. For example, in Fig. 19.12 the key is the animal name and the data items are linked together in ascending order of animal name.

To maintain and update an ordered linked list we must be able to insert a new element in its correct logical position, delete an existing element and amend the contents of an existing element.

It follows, then, that for each of these requirements we need a procedure that will determine the position in the list of an element with a given key value and whether or not that key value already exists in the list.

A general-purpose algorithm to

```
Find the position where the element should be
```

is now given:

```
Get list head position as current element
Initialize predecessor position to NULL
Initialize already exists indicator to 0
WHILE not end of list
      and specified key > current key in list
   Set predecessor position to current position
   Get next position in list as current element
IF specified key = current key
   Set already exists to 1
```

Consider a linked list with the key values

```
4   6   10   17   22
```

and suppose we want to find the position for a key value of 15. The WHILE loop would terminate when the specified key is less than or equal to the current key (17); at this stage, predecessor will contain the position of the item with value 10. In this case the already exists indicator would retain the value 0. However, given a value of 17, the loop would again terminate with predecessor containing the

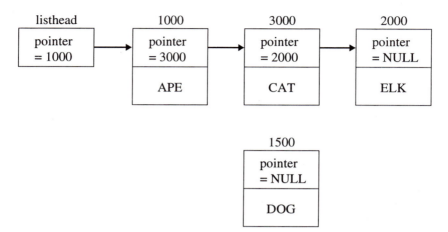

Figure 19.13

position of the item with the value 10, but this time the already exists indicator would be set to the value 1.

The above outline will also work with a specified key of 25 to be inserted at the end of the list, and for a key value of 2 to be inserted at the list head, in which case predecessor would hold NULL.

Algorithms for inserting a new element, deleting an existing element and amending an existing element are now considered. In each case we first use the above algorithm to obtain the position of the predecessor and an indicator showing whether or not the key already exists.

Algorithm 1 To insert an element

Consider the ordered list and the new element DOG to be added to it, as given in Fig. 19.13. We need to arrange for DOG to point to ELK, using the pointer obtained from CAT, the predecessor of DOG, and then change the pointer of CAT to point to DOG. This is illustrated in Fig. 19.14.

The pseudocode to insert an element is

```
Find the position where the element should be put
IF not a duplicate entry (key not already in list)
    Get memory for new element
    Assign data to new element
    IF insertion at beginning of list
        Make new element point to element currently at
            head of list
        Make listhead point to new element
    ELSE
        Make new element point to successor
```

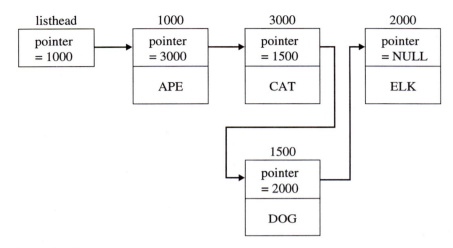

Figure 19.14

```
        Make predecessor point to new element
ELSE
    Report attempt to insert a duplicate key
```

Algorithm 2 To delete an element

To delete CAT from the revised list in Fig. 19.14, all that is necessary is to change the pointer of its predecessor (APE) such that it points to its successor (DOG) using the pointer currently held in CAT. This is shown diagrammatically in Fig. 19.15. Notice that the element CAT is now detached from the list and its memory may be returned to heap storage.

A general algorithm for deleting an element that allows for the element being at the start of the list is now given.

```
Find the position where the element should be
IF the specified item exists
    IF item is at the beginning of the list
        Make temporary element point to element currently
            at head of list
        Make listhead point to next item in the list
    ELSE
        Make temporary element point to predecessor's
            next item
        Make predecessor point to temporary element's
            successor
    Release memory using temporary element
ELSE
    Report attempt to delete missing item
```

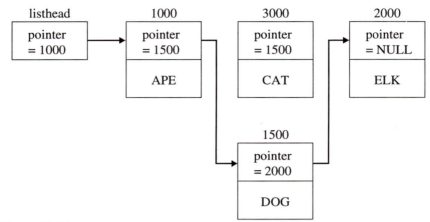

Figure 19.15

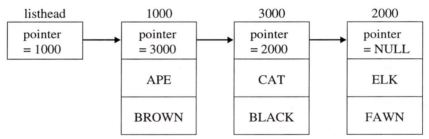

Figure 19.16

Algorithm 3 To amend the contents of an existing element

Now consider a similar linked list but with an additional member in its elements. This is given as Fig. 19.16.

Suppose we wish to change the colour of CAT to WHITE. Since the general search algorithm given above identifies the predecessor of the element that needs changing, we access its successor, giving the following pseudocode.

```
Find the position where the element should be
IF specified item exists in list
    IF item is at the beginning of the list
        Change data in element at head of list
    ELSE
        Change data in item next to predecessor
ELSE
    Report attempt to amend missing item.
```

A complete program using the above algorithms is now given in Figs 19.17 to 19.21. Each line of the file ANIMAL_1.DAT contains the name, which can be used as the key, and colour of an animal. The main program function (Fig. 19.17)

```
/* Demonstrates an ordered linked list */
#include <stdio.h>
#include <stdlib.h>
#include <string.h>
    typedef char STRING9 [9] ;
    struct beast
        {
        struct  beast *next ;
        STRING9 name,
                colour ;
        } ;
    typedef struct beast *LINK ;
    LINK list_head = NULL ;
    void find_position (STRING9, LINK *, int *) ;

main ()
{
/* Description  ......
    Read animal_1 file and create linked list
    Read animal_2 file and update list
    Read updated list and output to screen
*/
    LINK    element ;
    STRING9 name,
            colour ;
    char    code ;
    FILE    *animal_1 = fopen ("animal_1.dat", "r") ;
    FILE    *animal_2 = fopen ("animal_2.dat", "r") ;
    void insert_animal (STRING9, STRING9) ;
    void delete_animal (STRING9) ;
    void amend_animal (STRING9, STRING9) ;

    fscanf (animal_1, "%s%s", name, colour) ;
    while (feof (animal_1) == 0)
        {
        insert_animal (name, colour) ;
        fscanf (animal_1, "%s%s", name, colour) ;
        }
    fclose (animal_1) ;
    fscanf (animal_2, "%s%s %c", name, colour, &code) ;
    while (feof (animal_2) == 0)
        {
        switch (code)
            {
            case 'I'  :  insert_animal (name, colour) ;
                         break ;
            case 'D'  :  delete_animal (name) ;
                         break ;
            case 'A'  :  amend_animal (name, colour) ;
                         break ;
```

Figure 19.17

```
                default    :  printf ("Bad code : %s %c\n", name, code) ;
                }
           fscanf (animal_2, "\n%s%s %c", name, colour, &code) ;
           }
      fclose (animal_2) ;
      element = list_head ;
      while (element != NULL)
           {
           printf ("%s %s\n", element->name, element->colour) ;
           element = element->next ;
           }
}
```

Figure 19.17   Continued.

```
/* Function to find position of specified key in list.   */
/* position will hold the predecessor item or NULL if at */
/* list head. Flags if key already exists (exists = 1).  */

void find_position (STRING9 key, LINK *position, int *exists)
{
/* Description  ......
   Get list head position as current element
   Initialize predecessor position to NULL
   Initialize already exists indicator to 0
   WHILE not end of list and specified key > current key in list
       Set predecessor position to current position
       Get next position in list as current element
   IF specified key = current_key
       Set already exists to 1
*/
   LINK element = list_head ;

   *position = NULL ;
   *exists = 0 ;
   while ((element != NULL) && (strcmp (key, element->name) > 0))
       {
       *position = element ;
       element = element->next ;
       }
   if (strcmp (key, element->name) == 0)
       *exists = 1 ;
}
```

Figure 19.18

first creates an ordered linked list from this file using the function
`insert_animal` (Fig. 19.19).

Each line of a second file ANIMAL_2.DAT contains the animal name, colour
and a code for the type of transaction required. Valid codes are:

- I   Insert a new animal.
- D   Delete an existing animal.
- A   Amend an existing animal's colour.

The main program updates the linked list from this file using the appropriate
functions, `insert_animal` (Fig. 19.19), `delete_animal` (Fig. 19.20) or
`amend_animal` (Fig. 19.21). The updated linked list is then displayed on the
screen.

Fig. 19.18 contains the function `find_position` which is used by
`insert_animal`, `delete_animal` and `amend_animal`.

Exercises

1. Refer to the stack in Fig. 19.6.
   (i) Draw a revised diagram to show the addition of one more element with a
   data value of 175.
   (ii) Revise the diagram again to show the state of the stack after the removal of
   two elements.
2. Using the program shown in Fig. 19.7 (and given on disk as EX1901.C) as a
   basis, write a program to prompt for and read a string from the keyboard and
   then display each of its characters in reverse order. Assume that a string will
   never exceed 20 characters including the terminating null. If you need it, an
   outline design is available in EX1902.C (with appropriate cheats).
3. Amend your answer to question 2 to build a new string in the reverse order to
   that in which it is read. Then compare the original string with its reverse to see
   if the string is a palindrome and display an appropriate message. Examples of
   palindromes are ROTOR and 12321, that is they read the same backwards as
   they do forwards. An outline design is available in EX1903.C together with
   cheats if required.
4. Examine the program given in Figs 19.17 to 19.21, then answer the following
   questions:
   (i) What changes would you need to make to amend the list order from
   ascending order to descending order? That is, instead of APE being the first
   and ZEBRA the last, ZEBRA would be first and APE last.
   (ii) What amendment should you make to test that the allocation of memory has
   been successful?
   (iii) Draw a diagram to show the state of the ordered linked list immediately
   before and immediately after the last remaining element has been deleted.
   (iv) Describe the purpose of the `predecessor` pointer in each of the

functions `insert_animal`, `delete_animal` and `amend_animal`.

(v) As mentioned in the text, `find_position` is a general purpose function that returns `position`, a pointer to the predecessor of the specified key, and `exists`, an integer indicating whether or not the key already exists in the list.

It could be argued that for the `amend_animal` function it is better to use a function `find_key_position` that just returns `position`. In this case `position` will be a pointer to the element specified by the given key provided that it exists, otherwise NULL.

Write the function `find_key_position` and a new version of `amend_animal` that uses this new function.

5. Amend the program shown in Figs 19.17 to 19.21 (and given on disk as EX1904.C) to incorporate a new function that will count the occurrences of a given colour in the linked list and display this total with appropriate text and the given colour. The specification of the `animal_2` file would be changed to allow lines with an animal name of X followed by the given colour followed by a transaction code of C. The main program should call the new function whenever the transaction code of C is encountered.

An outline design is available for the amended program in EX1905.C. Cheats are also provided.

```
/* Function inserts a record into list in name order */

void insert_animal (STRING9 insert_name, STRING9 insert_colour)
{
/* Description  ......
   Find position where the element should be put
   IF not a duplicate entry (key not already in list)
      Get memory for new element
      Assign data to new element
      IF insertion at beginning of list
         Make new element point to element currently at head
         Make listhead point to new element
      ELSE
         Make new element point to successor
         Make predecessor point to new element
   ELSE
      Report attempt to insert a duplicate key
*/
   LINK new_ref,
        predecessor ;
   int  duplicate ;
```

Figure 19.19

```
    find_position (insert_name, &predecessor, &duplicate) ;
    if (duplicate != 1)
        {
        new_ref = malloc (sizeof (struct beast)) ;
        strcpy (new_ref->name, insert_name) ;
        strcpy (new_ref->colour, insert_colour) ;
        if (predecessor == NULL)
            {
            new_ref->next = list_head ;
            list_head = new_ref ;
            }
        else
            {
            new_ref->next = predecessor->next ;
            predecessor->next = new_ref ;
            }
        }
    else
        printf ("Duplicate insertion attempt : %s\n", insert_name) ;
}
```

Figure 19.19   Continued.

```
/* Function deletes a record from list for a given name */

void delete_animal (STRING9 delete_name)
{
/* Description  ......
    Find the position where the element should be
    IF the specified item exists
        IF item is at the beginning of the list
            Make temporary element point to element currently at head
            Make listhead point to next item in the list
        ELSE
            Make temporary element point to predecessor's next item
            Make predecessor point to temporary element's successor
        Release memory using temporary element
    ELSE
        Report attempt to delete missing item
*/
    LINK temp_element,
         predecessor ;
    int  located ;
```

Figure 19.20

```
   find_position (delete_name, &predecessor, &located) ;
   if (located == 1)
      {
      if (predecessor == NULL)
         {
         temp_element = list_head ;
         list_head = list_head->next ;
         }
      else
         {
         temp_element = predecessor->next ;
         predecessor->next = temp_element->next ;
         }
      free (temp_element) ;
      }
   else
      printf ("Deletion item not found : %s\n", delete_name) ;
}
```

Figure 19.20   Continued.

```
/* Function to amend the colour in a selected record */

void amend_animal (STRING9 amend_name, STRING9 amend_colour)
{
/* Description  ......
   Find the position where the element should be
   IF specified item exists in list
      IF item is at the beginning of the list
         Change data in element at head of list
      ELSE
         Change data in item next to predecessor
   ELSE
      Report attempt to amend missing item.
*/
   LINK predecessor ;
   int  located ;

   find_position (amend_name, &predecessor, &located) ;
   if (located == 1)
      {
      if (predecessor == NULL)
         strcpy (list_head->colour, amend_colour) ;
      else
         strcpy (predecessor->next->colour, amend_colour) ;
      }
   else
      printf ("Amendment item not found : %s\n", amend_name) ;
}
```

Figure 19.21

Appendix 1

Solutions to exercises

Chapter 2

1. `velocity` is valid
   `freda` is valid
   `time-of-day` is not valid because it contains hyphens
   `int` is not valid because it is a keyword.
   `tax_rate` is valid
   `x2` is valid
   `4x` is not valid because it starts with a digit

2. The first `printf` gives:

   3 3

   The second `printf` gives:

   7

3. The correct program is:

```
#include <stdio.h>
main ()
{
    int    anumber,
           bnumber,
           cnumber ;

/* The program starts here */
```

```
    anumber = 13 ;
    bnumber = 12 ;
    bnumber = anumber + bnumber ;
    cnumber = bnumber ;
    printf ("%d %d %d\n", anumber, bnumber, cnumber) ;
}
```

NB: The comment is incorrect and misleading and should be omitted.
4. Can be constructed by using EX0204.C and cheats 1–3.

Chapter 3

1. (i)   27 / 8 gives 3
   (ii)   27 % 5 gives 2
   (iii) − 27 * 3 gives −81
   (iv)   − 27 * 3 + 4 gives −77
   (v)   2 * 17 / (3 + 2) % 4 gives 2
   (vi)   3(2 − 9) is invalid because of a missing multiplication operator before the open parenthesis.
   (vii) 5 * ++ 3 / 4 gives 5

Statement number	varone	vartwo
1	3	
2		6
3		13
4	128	
5		33
6	15876	

Figure A1.3.1

2. See Fig. A1.3.1
   The resultant output is

   ```
   5 -2 15876 33
   ```

3. Can be constructed by using EX0303.C and cheats 6–10.
4. Can be constructed by using EX0304.C and cheats 11–14.

Chapter 4

1. answer = (2 * a + 4 * c) / (3 * b) ;

2. The output from the first `printf` is:

   ■ ■ ■ `41.570 79.34` (where ■ represents a space)

   The output from the second `printf` is:

   `325.7 0.0047`

3. Can be constructed by using EX0403.C and cheats 16-20.
4. Can be constructed by using EX0404.C and cheats 21-24.

Chapter 5

1. (i)   At the lines containing the `scanf` statements.
   (ii) The lines containing the first and third `printf` statements.
   (iii) `1.3` and `2.5`
   (iv) Because there is a space at the end of the control string in the `printf` statement.
   (v)   `Please type a number`
         `1.3`
         `This number squared is:    1.690`
         etc.
2. (i)   `*bhinp` and `*resout`
   (ii) The second argument of `fopen` is `"r"` for an input file and `"w"` for an output file.
   (iii) The identifier `bhinp` is used as a file pointer within the C program, whereas `bhinp.dat` is the name and extension of the file as known to the operating system.
   (iv) We could have a number of files open for input and/or ouput. We need to specify which of the files we wish to read from or write to.
   (v)   So that the reader can interpret the output in relation to the input. The reader may not have a copy of the input.
   (vi) By comparing them with some manually calculated results.
   (vii) By using an editor program.
3. Can be constructed by using EX0503.C and cheats 25–28.
4. Can be constructed by using EX0504.C and cheats 29–37.
5. Can be constructed by using EX0505.C and cheats 38–44.

Chapter 6

1. (i)   To allow for a space to separate this text from the preceding value (that is, the value of `commission_rate`) that is displayed on the same line. Note there is no \n in the previous `printf` statement.
   (ii) Ideally at least three: one where the commission is less than 10, one where it is equal to 10 and one where it is greater than 10.

(iii) Because we cannot guarantee exact representation of some real numbers. An equality test might give false when it should be true because of rounding errors.

2. (i)   True.
    (ii) True.
    (iii) True.
    (iv) True.
    (v)   False.
    (vi) True.

3. Can be constructed by using EX0603.C and cheats 45–50.
4. Can be constructed by using EX0604.C and cheats 52–55.
5. Can be constructed by using EX0605.C and cheats 56–63.
6. Can be constructed by using EX0606.C and cheats 64–69.

Chapter 7

1. (i)   `(current_number != 9999)`
    (ii) If the first number read was the end marker then there would be a count of zero. Using the count as a divisor to produce the mean would give a division by zero. This is not posssible, and produces an error at run time.
    (iii) The while loop would continue indefinitely processing the first value read.
    (iv) As the initial contents of the variable `current_number` is undefined, unpredictable results would follow.

2. (i)   Simply change the constant value of `last_value` to 20.
    (ii) Change `last_value` to 20.
          Change the first assignment statement to:

          ```
          current_number = 2 ;
          ```

          to start at the first even number.
          Change the third assignment statement to:

          ```
          current_number += 2 ;
          ```

          to get the next even number.
    (iii) This will give a completely blank line under the heading line.

3. (i)   None at all. They are logically equivalent.
    (ii) Change all occurrences of `largest` to `smallest`.
          Change the `if` statement as follows:

          ```
          if (current_value < smallest)
          ```

          Change the `printf` appropriately.
    (iii) At its declaration with a number known to be smaller than all those in the list (or, to be precise, smaller than the first one in the list):

```
int largest = -99999 ;
```

or, similarly by an assignment statement.

4. (i) The first fscanf is part of the read-ahead technique. If the file just contains the end marker, the main loop would not be entered.

(ii) number_of_readings is incremented by one for every reading in a set. The set could have no readings, so the variable must be set to zero. total_readings is accumulated within the loop from current_reading. It must be initialized to zero for each set of readings because there may be no readings for a set and zero is the correct value before any readings are added to it.

5. Can be constructed by using EX0705.C and cheats 70–78.
6. Can be constructed by using EX0706.C and cheats 79–89.
7. Can be constructed by using EX0707.C and cheats 90–99.
8. Can be constructed by using EX0708.C and cheats 100–114.

Chapter 8

1. (i) True.
   (ii) False.
   (iii) True.
   (iv) False.
   (v) True.
   (vi) False.
2. (i) No, because this would mean that any character that was not a capital letter (e.g. punctuation marks) would be counted as a digit.
   (ii) The output would be:

```
AB ?1X4 5+E;
There are 4 capital letters and 3 digits
```

3. (i) Because we are using the function strcmp.
   (ii) That line would be processed as a normal data line and ouput as:

```
First string is 'ZZZZZ'
Second string is 'XXXXX'
```

Note that for the program to be terminated correctly a final line of ZZZZZ ZZZZZ is needed.

(iii) The fscanf statements would be:

```
fscanf (inpfile, "%s%s%s", first_string,
    second_string, third_string) ;
```

third_string would need to be declared:

```
char third_string [6] ;
```

A further `printf` statement is needed:

```
printf ("Third string is '%s'\n", third_string) ;
```

If we assume that all three strings must be ZZZZZ for the program to terminate correctly, the `while` statement must be changed to:

```
while (! ((strcmp (first_string, "ZZZZZ") == 0) &&
       (strcmp (second_string, "ZZZZZ") == 0) &&
       (strcmp (third_string, "ZZZZZ") == 0)))
```

4. Can be constructed by using EX0804.C and cheats 126-135.
5. Can be constructed by using EX0805.C and cheats 136-150.
6. Can be constructed by using EX0806.C and cheats 173-181.

Chapter 9

```
1. #include <stdio.h>
   main ()
   {
       const int outer_initial = 10,
                 outer_final = 13,
                 inner_initial = 100,
                 inner_final = 102 ;
       int outer_counter,
           inner_counter ;

       outer_counter = outer_initial ;
       while (outer_counter <= outer_final)
          {
          inner_counter = inner_initial ;
          while (inner_counter <= inner_final)
             {
             printf ("%3d %3d\n", outer_counter,
                 inner_counter) ;
             ++ inner_counter ;
             }
          ++ outer_counter ;
          }
   }
```

```
2. (i)  Group is 4
   (ii) 6
        Group is 0
   (iii) Group is 3
```

(iv) 1
    `Group is 1`
(v) `Group is 4`
(vi) −1
    `Group is 0`

3. Can be constructed by using EX0903.C and cheats 196–199.
4. Can be constructed by using EX0904.C and cheats 206–210.
5. Can be constructed by using EX0905.C and cheats 211–216.
6. Can be constructed by using EX0906.C and cheats 218–223.
7. Can be constructed by using EX0907.C and cheats 224–237.

Chapter 10

1. (i) The local identifiers of the function are `number` and `sum`.
   (ii) The parameters of the function are `first` and `last`.
   (iii) The arguments of the function calls are `firsta` and `lasta` in the first
        call, and `firstb` and `lastb` in the second call.
        The variable `sum` is necessary as a local variable in the function to hold an
        intermediate and final result.
2. `swapa (&argument_a, &argument_b)` will cause the value 4 to be
   placed in `argument_b` and 2 in `argument_a`.
   `swapb (argument_a, argument_b)` will have no effect on the values
   in `argument_a` and `argument_b` because only the values of these
   arguments are passed to the function.
3. Can be constructed by using EX1003.C and cheat 242.
4. Can be constructed by using EX1004.C and cheats 243–248.
5. Can be constructed by using EX1005.C and cheats 249–260.
6. Can be constructed by using EX1006.C and cheats 261–266.
7. Can be constructed by using EX1007.C and cheats 267–270.
8. Can be constructed by using EX1008.C and cheats 271–285.

Chapter 11

1. It may be easy to assume that our results are correct by casually glancing at
   them. If we produce expected results in advance of executing a test case, we
   will more likely discipline ourselves to be thorough in checking the results.
2. A relational expression may be compound. In such cases there may be a variety
   of possible combinations leading to both true and false. We should provide test
   data that take this into account.

3. We might introduce an error while in the process of correcting another error. We can help to guard against this by retesting with all previous test data cases.

4. (i) Insert after line 1:

```
#include <stdio.h>
```

Line 12 should be:

```
float sum,        (comma instead of semicolon)
```

Line 24 has a missing &, it should be:

```
fscanf (ex1104, "%f", &delimiter) ;
```

Line 34 has missing parentheses, it should be:

```
if (number > largest)
```

Line 41 has a missing ", it should be:

```
printf ("Summary of results\n") ;
```

Insert a right brace after final `printf`.

(ii)   Welcome to AVSSP

```
                 1 23.40
                 2 16.90
                 3 25.05
                 4 111.70
                 5 20.40
Summary of results
Number of data items = 5
Average is : 39.49
Maximum is : 111.70
Minimum is : 16.90
   Range is : 94.80
```

(iii) The `fscanf` statement at line 29 should be placed two lines earlier before the assignment to `smallest`. The `while` statement at line 30 should be:

```
while (number != delimiter)
```

There is a missing `fscanf` statement in the loop. The following should be inserted immediately before the right brace at line 40:

```
fscanf (ex1104, "%f", &number) ;
```

The relational operator in line 36 should be changed to `<`.

5. No solution is provided for this exercise.

Chapter 12

1.

```
Step 1
   Prepare files and read first record
   Initialize count (=0)
   WHILE not end of file
      Process a record
   Write count
   Close files

Step 2
   Prepare files and read first record
   Initialize count (=0)
   WHILE not end of file
      IF due for replacement
         Increase count by 1
      Write duplicate record
      Read next record
   Write count
   Close files
```

2.

```
Step 1
   Prepare files and read first record
   WHILE not end of file
      Process a ward
   Close files

Step 2
   Prepare files and read first record
   WHILE not end of file
      Write ward headings
      Store ward code
      WHILE not at end of ward
         Process a record
   Close files

Step 3
   Prepare files and read first record
   WHILE not end of file
      Write ward headings
      Store ward code
      WHILE not at end of ward
         IF a staff member
            Write name of staff member
         Read next record
   Close files
```

3.

```
Step 1
   Prepare files and read first record
   WHILE not end of file
      Process an area
   Close files

Step 2
   Prepare files and read first record
   WHILE not end of file
      Store area code
      Initialize area total (=0)
      WHILE not end of area
         Process a district
      Write area total
   Close files

Step 3
   Prepare files and read first record
   WHILE not end of file
      Store area code
      Initialize area total (=0)
      WHILE not end of area
         Store district code
         Initialize district total (=0)
         WHILE not end of district
            IF required product
               Add to area and district totals
            Read next record
         Write district total
      Write area total
   Close files
```

4.

```
Step 1
   Prepare files and read first record
   WHILE not end of file
      Process a course
   Close files

Step 2
   Prepare files and read first record
   WHILE not end of file
      Write course headings
      Store course code
      Initialize course total (=0)
```

```
      Process offered applicants
      Process rejected applicants
      Write course total
   Close files

Step 3
   Prepare files and read first record
   WHILE not end of file
      Write course headings
      Store course code
      Initialize course total (=0)
      WHILE not rejected students for current course
         Read next record
      WHILE not end of course
         Increase course total by 1
         Write applicant's name
         Read next record
      Write course total
   Close files
```

Chapter 13

1. (i) Before the second `for` statement, add:

```
printf ("Salesmen Achieving Bonus Level\n\n") ;
printf ("Ref.  Sales\n") ;
```

and amend the `printf` statement to include more spaces between the reference number and the sales figure.

(ii) Declare the new `int` variable `index_of_best`.
Before either loop include

```
index_of_best = 0 ;
```

and then within the corresponding loop include

```
if (sales [index] > sales [index_of_best])
   index_of_best = index ;
```

At the end of the program include

```
printf ("\nBest salesman is no. %d\n",
   index_of_best + 1) ;
```

(iii) Declare new `int` variables `counter` and `ref_number`, change the first `for` statement as follows:

```
for (counter = 0 ; counter < SALESMEN ;
   ++ counter)
   {
```

```
fscanf (salesfile, "%d%f", &ref_number,
    &sales [ref_number - 1]) ;
total_sales += sales [ref_number - 1] ;
    }
```

2. We could restrict the search by stopping it when the target value is found or is less than an element of the table. There would be no point in continuing from this point because a match can no longer be found.

3. `int primes [10] = {1, 2, 3, 5, 7, 11, 13, 17, 19, 23};`

```
char roman [8] = "IVXLDCM" ; or
char roman [8] = {'I', 'V', 'X', 'L', 'D', 'C', 'M'} ;
```

4. Can be constructed by using EX1304.C and cheats 301–307.
5. Can be constructed by using EX1305.C and cheats 308–318.
6. Can be constructed by using EX1306.C and cheats 321–327.
7. Can be constructed by using EX1307.C and cheats 328–335.

Chapter 14

1. (i) The initialization of the array is done when the array is declared. Note that only one zero is specified in the braces; all other elements will be filled with zeros automatically.
   (ii) No solution provided.
2. Can be constructed by using EX1402.C and cheats 350–359.
3. Can be constructed by using EX1403.C and cheats 361–365.
4. Can be constructed by using EX1404.C and cheats 366–373.

Chapter 15

1. Without enumerated types the program would be less clear to the human reader, because the program would probably refer to integers 1 to 5 rather than to easily recognized names.

2. (i) `enum faculties {Science, Medicine, Law,`
   `                  Engineering} ;`
   `    enum faculties faculty ;`

   (ii)
```
scanf (inpfile, "%c", &character) ;
switch (character)
    {
    case 'S' : faculty = Science ;
            break ;
    case 'M' : faculty = Medicine ;
            break ;
```

```
      case 'L' : faculty = Law ;
                 break ;
      case 'E' : faculty = Engineering ;
                 break ;
      }
```

3. Declare an enumerated type such as

```
enum days_of_week {Monday, Tuesday, Wednesday,
      Thursday, Friday, Saturday, Sunday} ;
```

Replace the declaration of `loop_control` by

```
enum  days_of_week day ;
```

Amend the `for` statement as follows:

```
for (day = Monday ; day <= Sunday ; ++ day)
    {
    scanf ("%d", &hours) ;
    switch (day)
        {
        Saturday  : rate = base_rate * 1.5 ;
                     break ;
        Sunday    : rate = base_rate * 2 ;
                     break ;
        default   : rate = base_rate ;
        }
    wages += hours * rate ;
    }
```

4.
```
typedef  int MARK_TABLE [STUDENTS] [PAPERS],
             int STUDENT,
             int PAPER ;

  MARK_TABLE marks = { 0 } ;
  STUDENT    student_index,
             student_total,
             student_number ;
  PAPER      paper_index,
             paper_number ;
```

Chapter 16

1. (i)   1
   (ii) 1996
   (iii) not valid
   (iv) not valid

2. (i) `person_table [4]`
   (ii) `person_table [9].name.forenames [2]`

3. (i)
```
struct part_record
    {
    int    part_number ;
    char   part_name [10] ;
    float price ;
    } ;

struct part_record one_part,
                    second_part ;
```

   (ii)
```
one_part.part_number = 20 ;
strcpy (one_part.part_name, "SOCKET") ;
one_part.price = 4.12 ;
second_part = one_part ;
```

   (iii)
```
if (one_part.part_number < 25)
    one_part.price = 2 * one_part.price ;
else
    one_part.price = 3 * one_part.price ;
printf ("%d\n", second_part.part_number) ;
printf ("%s\n", second_part.part_name) ;
printf ("%.2f\n", second_part.price) ;
```

4. Can be constructed by using EX1604.C and cheats 385-389.

5.
```
#define CITIES 20

struct city_struct
    {
    char name [21] ;
    char code ;
    int  population ;
    }
struct city_struct city [CITIES] ;
```

We would access the name of the fifth city by
`city [4].name`

6. (i)
```
#define PEOPLE 30
struct fullname
    {
    char surname [21] ;
    char initials [5] ;
    } ;
struct date
```

```
        {
        int day,
            month,
            year ;
        } ;
    struct person_struct
        {
        struct fullname name ;
        struct date join_date ;
        } ;
    struct person_struct group [PEOPLE] ;
```

(ii) (a) `strcpy (group [5].name.surname, "Brown") ;`
`strcpy (group [5].name.initials, "RWS") ;`
(b) `strcpy (group [3].name.surname, "Williams") ;`
(c) `group [9].join_date.month = 11 ;`
(d) `group [11].join_date.day = 21 ;`
`group [11].join_date.month = 3 ;`
`group [11].join_date.year = 1984 ;`

Chapter 17

1. (i) Will cause a string of characters of any length to be read from the file referenced by `file_pointer` up to a space, newline or tab character. The string will be stored starting at the start of the variable `string_variable` with no check to see if the variable is large enough to hold the string. A null character will be added to the end of the string.

   (ii) Will cause up to 24 characters including space characters to be read from the file referenced by `file_pointer`. The process will be stopped if a newline character or end of file is read. A null character is added to the end of the string.

2. Can be constructed by using EX1702.C and cheats 390–399.

3. Can be constructed by using EX1703.C and cheats 400–407.

4. Can be constructed by using EX1704.C and cheats 408–424.

Chapter 18

```
1. #define ARRAY_MAX 12
   #define START 12
   int numbers [ARRAY_MAX] ;
   int count ;

   for (count = START ; count < START + ARRAY_MAX ;
        ++ count)
        numbers [count - START] = count ;
```

2. `result = ((y + 8 / z) * (y + 8 / z)) + x ;`
3. `error = 5 + ((x + 3) * (x + 3))*x + 3 ;`
   This would give an incorrect result because $(x + 3)^2$ would be multipled by x then 3 added to that result. Parentheses would be required around the third y in the macro definition, giving

   `CUBE(y)  SQR(y)*(y)`

4. Can be constructed by using EX1804.C and cheats 430–438 together with EX1805.C, EX1805.H, EX1802.C and EX1803.C.

Chapter 19

1. (i)

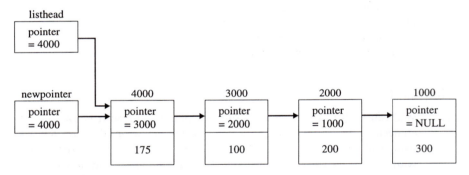

Figure A1.19.1

(ii)

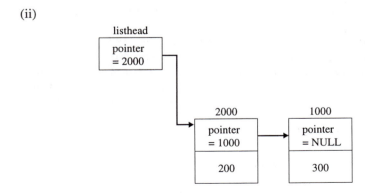

Figure A1.19.2

2. Can be constructed by using EX1902.C and cheats 440–452.
3. Can be constructed by using EX1903.C and cheats 460–470.
4. (i) In function `find_position` change the relational operator in the `while` statement from > to <.

   (ii) In function `insert` after the call to function `malloc` add the following code:

```
if (new_ref == NULL)
    {
    printf ("Unable to allocate memory\n") ;
    exit (1) ;
    }
```

(iii)

Before removal of last element

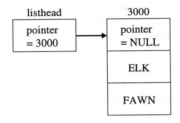

After removal of last element

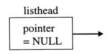

Figure A1.19.3

(iv) In function `insert_animal`, the `predecessor` pointer has two purposes. First, if it is NULL, the insertion is to be at the head of the list. Second, the `next` pointer of the predecessor needs to contain the address of the inserted element. In function `delete_animal`, the `predecessor` pointer also has two purposes. First, if it is NULL, the deletion is from the head of the list, so the `list_head` pointer needs to be altered. Second, the `next` pointer of the predecessor has to be altered to point to the element after the one being removed. In function `amend_animal`, again there are two purposes for the `predecessor` pointer. First, if it is NULL, the element at the head of the list is changed. Second, the element pointed to by the `next` pointer of the predecessor is the one to be changed.

(v)

```
/* Function to find position of specified key in list.  */
/* If not found NULL is returned                        */

void find_key_position (STRING9 key, LINK *position)
{
/* Description ......
   Get list head position as current element
   Initialize position to NULL
   WHILE not end of list and specified key > current key in list
      Get next position in list as current element
   IF specified key = current_key
      Make position point to current element
*/
   LINK element = list_head ;

   *position = NULL ;
   while ((element != NULL) && (strcmp (key, element->name) > 0))
      element = element->next ;
   if (strcmp (key, element->name) == 0)
      *position = element ;
}


/* Revised function to amend the colour of a selected record */

void amend_animal (STRING9 amend_name, STRING9 amend_colour)
{
/* Description ......
   Find the position where the element should be
   IF specified item exists in list
      Change data in item at key position
   ELSE
      Report attempt to amend missing item.
*/
   LINK key_position ;

   find_key_position (amend_name, &key_position) ;
   if (key_position != NULL)
      strcpy (key_position->colour, amend_colour) ;
   else
      printf ("Amendment item not found : %s\n", amend_name) ;
}
```

Figure A1.19.4

5. Can be constructed by using EX1905.C and cheats 480–484.

Appendix 2

An exercise using an editor program

The detailed instructions that are given are for two editors that you may have: Microsoft's MS-DOS editor and Borland's editor from its integrated development environments (such as Borland C++). Where the commands are the same no qualification is given; but where they are different, both commands are shown suitably designated.

1. Getting started

1. The purpose of this exercise is to change the file EDITX.TXT, so that it is identical to EDITA.TXT, (see Fig. A2.9.1). Make a copy of each of these files on your own disk. They are to be found in the EXERCISE directory on the supplied disk.
2. Check that these files are on your disk and view the contents of the files.
3. Start your editor and retrieve your copy of the file EDITX.TXT.

2. Moving the cursor

1. Use the four arrow keys to move the cursor around the screen.
2. Place the cursor in the middle of the screen then move it to the beginning and end of a line by:
   pressing the keys marked <HOME> and <END> respectively.
3. Place the cursor at the start of a line of text then move it to the right, one word at a time, by:
   holding down the key marked <CTRL> and pressing the <RIGHT ARROW> key.
   There are many editor functions that are effected by holding down the <CTRL> key or the <SHIFT> key while pressing another key. We will describe such

actions by 'press <CTRL> and <X> keys' or 'press <SHIFT> and <X> keys'.

3. Deleting text

1. The backspace-and-delete key is useful when you make a typing error as it deletes the character to the left of the cursor. Type the word rubbish anywhere in the file and then delete it.
2. The key marked <DEL> deletes the character on which the cursor is sitting. Use it to delete the ' ' ' and $$$ in the second verse.
3. Pressing <CTRL> and <T> deletes the current word. Use it to delete the words sometimes and nearly in the second verse. First ensure that the cursor is at the start of the required word. Delete the space following each of these words if necessary.
4. Pressing <CTRL> and <Y> deletes the current line. Use it to delete the four lines identified in verse one.

4. Inserting text

Editors may be in 'insert' mode (the most commonly used) or 'overstrike' mode. In overstrike mode, typing overwrites characters at the cursor position. In insert mode, typing inserts characters at the cursor position. For the most part we need to be in insert mode. We do this in most editors by pressing the <INS> key. This key acts like a toggle; we press it once we are in overstrike mode, we press it again and we are in insert mode. Before continuing, press <INS> and test which mode you are in. Make sure that you are in insert mode.

1. To insert text within a line simply type the text wherever you want it. Insert learnt and then times at the appropriate place in the penultimate line. Insert But at the start of the last line of the first verse.
2. Insert two rows of * * * * between the first and second verses and at the end of the second verse.
3. To insert new lines we have to open up a line initially and then use the <ENTER> key at the end of each line.
   (i)   Move the cursor to the start of the first line of the first verse.
   (ii) Press the <ENTER> key to give a blank line.
   (iii) Press the <ENTER> key again.
   (iv) Move cursor up one line.
   (v)   Insert BY M. E. ANDYOU and then press the <ENTER> key for another blank line.

5. Amending text using delete and insert

On the last line, delete `orange` and replace it with `bad`, delete `is` and replace it with `were`.

6. Moving and copying text

Before moving, duplicating or deleting blocks of text, we must first select the block of text required. This is achieved by different sequences depending on the editor used.

1. We will move the line containing THE END to the end of the file.
   For Borland's editor:
   (i)   Move the cursor to the start of the line containing THE END.
   (ii) Press <CTRL> and <K>, then press the <B> key. This marks the beginning of the selected block of text.
   (iii) Move the cursor to the start of the next line.
   (iv) Press <CTRL> and <K>, then press the <K> key. This marks the end of the selected block of text. The selected text will now be highlighted on the screen.
   (v)   Move the cursor to the end of the file so that it is positioned at the start of a new line (you may need to create this line by pressing the <ENTER> key).
   (vi) Press <CTRL> and <K>, then press the <V> key. The previously selected text should now be at the end of the file, highlighted as before.
   (vii) Press <CTRL> and <K>, then press the <H> key. The highlighting is turned off.
   For the MS-DOS editor:
   (i)   Move the cursor to the start of the line containing THE END.
   (ii) Press <SHIFT> and <down arrow>. This moves the cursor and highlights the line. Note that continuing to press these keys would highlight a number of lines as a block of text.
   (iii) Press <SHIFT> and <DEL>. This deletes the line but preserves a copy of it.
   (iv) Move the cursor to the end of the file so that it is positioned at the start of a new line.
   (v)   Press <SHIFT> and <INS>. The previously selected text should now be at the end of the file.
2. Now move the three lines of * * * * * * * from the top of the file to just before THE END.
   (i)   Move the cursor to the top of the file.
   (ii) Select the block of lines, as indicated in (1).
   (iii) Move the cursor to the required position (start of THE END line).
   (iv) Move the selected block.
3. Duplicate the first verse as the third verse.

For Borland's editor:

(i)   Move the cursor to the start of the first verse.

(ii) Press <CTRL> and <K>, then press the <B> key.

(iii) Move the cursor to the start of the line that follows the end of the first verse.

(iv) Press <CTRL> and <K>, then press the <K> key. The selected text will now be highlighted on the screen.

(v)   Move the cursor to where you want the third verse.

(vi) Press <CTRL> and <K>, then press the <C> key. The previously selected text should now be copied at the required position.

For the MS-DOS editor:

(i)   Move the cursor to the start of the first verse.

(ii) Press <SHIFT> and <down arrow> until the cursor is positioned at the start of the line following the end of the verse.

(iii) Press <CTRL> and <INS>. This makes a copy of the lines.

(iv) Move the cursor to where you want the third verse.

(v)   Press <SHIFT> and <INS>. The previously selected text should now be copied at the required position.

7. Replacing text

1. To replace all occurrences of the word bear in the third verse with the word boy, we use the following procedure.

Borland's editor:

(i)   Position the cursor at the top of the file.

(ii)   Press <CTRL> and <Q>.

(iii) Press the <A> key. You now see a menu of options.

(iv)   Type the word bear, then press the <TAB> key.

(v)   Type the word boy, then press the <TAB> key 6 times. You should now see the words Change all highlighted.

(vi)   Press the <ENTER> key. You will now be presented with a window with a question Replace this occurrence? in it and the word bear highlighted.

(vii) If the word bear is in the first or second verse type N. The question will be repeated.

(viii) Keep responding with N until the highlighted word bear is in the third verse, then respond by typing Y.

(ix)   Keep on responding with Y until the question is no longer asked.

For the MS-DOS editor:

(i)   Position the cursor at the top of the file.

(ii)   Press <CTRL> and <Q>.

(iii) Press the <A> key. You now see a window.

(iv)   Type the word bear, then press the <TAB> key.

A POEM

BY M. E. ANDYOU

```
There were two little bears who lived in a wood.
And one of them was bad and the other was good.
Good bear learnt his twice times one
But bad bear left all his buttons undone.
****
****
They lived in a tree when the weather was hot.
And one of them was good, and the other was not;
Good bear learnt his twice times two
But bad bear's thingummies were worn right through.
****
****
There were two little boys who lived in a wood.
And one of them was bad and the other was good.
Good boy learnt his twice times one
But bad boy left all his buttons undone.
              *******
              *******
              *******
              THE END
```

Figure A2.9.1   (with apologies to A. A. Milne)

(v)   Type the word boy, then press the <TAB> key 3 times. You should now see the words Find and Verify highlighted.

(vi) Press <ALT> and <V>. You will now be presented with a window with Change and Skip options and the word bear highlighted.

(vii) If the word bear is in the first or second verse press <ALT> and <S>. The window will remain there with a different occurrence of bear highlighted.

(viii) Keep responding with <ALT> and <S> until the highlighted word bear is in the third verse, then respond by typing <ALT> and <C>.

(ix) Keep on responding with <ALT> and <C> until the window is removed. Obviously, there are many options available in replacing text. You may like to experiment with them at your leisure.

8. Terminating the edit session

You should now save your file.

For Borland's editor:

By pressing the <F2> key.

For the MS-DOS editor:

By pressing <Alt> and <F>, followed by typing the <S> key.

9. Compare your EDITX.TXT with EDITA.TXT

If you have any software to compare the files (such as the MS-DOS `comp` command) this would be the quicker way; otherwise, print your amended file and compare it visually with the file given in Fig. A2.9.1. If the files are not the same then you might like to continue editing EDITX.TXT until it agrees with EDITA.TXT (see Fig. A2.9.1). Even if they are the same, continue using the editor until you can use the above facilities with confidence.

Index

#define, 139, 184
#include, 8, 183

Addition operator +, 17
Address operator &, 34, 99
    and logical operator &&, 44
Arguments of functions, 9, 93, 98
Arithmetic:
    floating point, 25
    integer, 17
    operators, 17, 25
Arrays:
    declaration, 138
    indexes (subscripts), 138, 146
    initializing, 141, 142, 146
    multi-dimensional, 145
    one-dimensional, 138
ASCII character codes, 69
Assignment operators, 8, 13
Assignment statements, 8, 13

Braces { }, 8, 49, 141
break, 86

case, 86
char, 66
Character codes, 69
Characters:
    reading, 67

writing, 68
Closing files, 37
Comments, 7, 9
Comparing strings, 73
Compilation, 4, 5
Compound expressions, 43
Compound statement, 49
const, 12
Constants:
    symbolic, 139, 184
Control string, 9, 19
Correctness, 122

Data, 2
Data structures:
    declaration, 169
    dynamic, 192
Data type:
    char, 66
    float, 24
    Fundamental, 157
    Integer, 17
Data types, 12
de Morgan's laws, 47
Debugging, 4, 116
Declarations:
    arrays, 138, 146, 151
    constant identifiers, 12
    type identifiers, 158

variable identifiers, 8, 13
Design:
   constructs, 124
   objectives, 123
Directives (preprocessor), 183
Division operator, 17
do-while, 83
Documentation, 123
double, 25, 94, 157
Dynamic data structures, 192

Editors, 5
Efficiency, 122
End of file, 179
enum, 159
Enumerated types, 159
EOF, 179
Equality operator ==, 42
Errors:
   logical, 4, 115
   run-time, 4
   syntax, 4, 114
exit, 177

fclose, 37, 175
feof, 179
fgetc, 178
fgets, 178
Field width, 19, 26
Files:
   closing, 37, 175
   opening, 36, 175, 176
   reading, 37, 175
   writing, 37, 175
float, 12, 24
fopen, 36, 175, 176
for, 80, 81
Formal parameters, 96
Format string, 19
fprintf, 37, 175
fputc, 177
fputs, 177
fscanf, 37, 175

Function:
   call, 9, 93
   definition, 95
   parameters (arguments), 98
   prototype, 95
Function header, 95
Fundamental data types, 157

getchar, 178
Greater than >, 42
Greater than or equal >=, 42

Header file, 176, 183
Heap, 194

Identifiers, 2, 12
if, 41
if-else, 41
Indirection operator *, 101
int, 8, 13
INT_MAX, 17
INT_MIN, 17
Integer arithmetic, 17
Integer output, 19
Interactive input and output, 34
Iteration, 55, 80, 124

Keyword, 8, 10

Less than <, 42
Less than or equal <=, 42
Linked lists, 205
Local identifiers, 97
Logical errors, 4, 115
Logical operators, 43
long, 17, 157
long double, 158

Macros, 185
main, 8
malloc, 194
math.h, 28
Member access operator, 165

Members, 164
Memory allocation, 194
Modifiability, 122
Multi-dimensional arrays, 145
Multiplication, 13
    operator, 17

Negation operator, 44
Nested control structures, 59
Nested selections, 48
Not equal ! =, 42
Not logical operator !, 44
NULL, 176
Null character \ 0, 70

Opening files, 36, 175
Operating systems, 5
Operators:
    arithmetic, 17
    assignment, 8, 13
    logical, 43
    or logical operator | |, 44
    precedence, 18
    relational, 42
Output of:
    integer values, 19
    real values, 26

Pointers, 35, 191
pow, 30
Precedence of operators, 18
Preprocessor, 8, 183
printf, 9, 32
Programming languages, 1
Prototypes (function), 95
Pseudocode, 125

Queues, 200

Read-ahead, 56
Reading from:
    files, 37
    the keyboard, 34

Real expressions, 25
Real numbers, 12
Relational operators, 42
Reliability, 122
Remainder operator %, 17
Repetition, 55
return, 96
Run-time errors, 4

Sample data, 131
Sample input file, 125, 127
scanf, 34
Scope (of identifiers), 105
Selection, 41, 124
Semicolon, 9
Sequence, 124
Signed char, 157
Simplicity, 122
sizeof, 194
sqrt, 28
Stack, 193
stdio.h, 8
strcmp, 73
strcpy, 71
Stream, 175
string.h, 71
Strings, 70, 142
struct, 164
Subscripts, 138
Subtraction, 17
Subtraction operator, 17
switch, 84
Symbolic constants, 139
Syntax errors, 4, 114

Table look-up, 141
Test data, 115
Testing, 114, 115
Trace table, 16
typedef, 158

Underscore, 9
union, 171

unsigned char, 157
Using data files, 35

Variables, 13
void, 98

while, 55
White space characters, 67
Writing to:
  files, 37
  the monitor screen, 32